Leading for Tomorrow's Schools Today

Leading for Tomorrow's Schools Today

Michael Lubelfeld

Nick Polyak

BLOOMSBURY ACADEMIC
NEW YORK • LONDON • OXFORD • NEW DELHI • SYDNEY

BLOOMSBURY ACADEMIC

Bloomsbury Publishing Inc, 1359 Broadway, 12th Floor, New York, NY 10018, USA
Bloomsbury Publishing Plc, 50 Bedford Square, London, WC1B 3DP, UK
Bloomsbury Publishing Ireland, 29 Earlsfort Terrace, Dublin 2, D02 AY28, Ireland

BLOOMSBURY, BLOOMSBURY ACADEMIC and the Diana logo are trademarks of
Bloomsbury Publishing Plc

First published in the United States of America 2026

Copyright © Michael Lubelfeld and Nick Polyak, 2026
AASA Logo © The School Superintendents Association (AASA)

Cover images © istock/Alena Butusava

All rights reserved. No part of this publication may be: i) reproduced or transmitted in any form, electronic or mechanical, including photocopying, recording or by means of any information storage or retrieval system without prior permission in writing from the publishers; or ii) used or reproduced in any way for the training, development or operation of artificial intelligence (AI) technologies, including generative AI technologies. The rights holders expressly reserve this publication from the text and data mining exception as per Article 4(3) of the Digital Single Market Directive (EU) 2019/790.

Bloomsbury Publishing Inc does not have any control over, or responsibility for, any third-party websites referred to or in this book. All internet addresses given in this book were correct at the time of going to press. The author and publisher regret any inconvenience caused if addresses have changed or sites have ceased to exist, but can accept no responsibility for any such changes.

A catalog record for this book is available from the Library of Congress.

ISBN: HB: 978-1-4758-7486-0
PB: 978-1-4758-7487-7
ePDF: 979-8-7651-6039-8
eBook: 978-1-4758-7488-4

Typeset by Deanta Global Publishing Services, Chennai, India
Printed and bound in the United States of America

For product safety related questions contact productsafety@bloomsbury.com.

To find out more about our authors and books visit www.bloomsbury.com
and sign up for our

Contents

Preface vii
Foreword *by Thomas C. Murray* xiv
Acknowledgments xvi

Introduction 1

Part I Leadership Is Change 7

1 Cultivating Change 9

2 Selection of Staff: Who, How, and How Long? 19

Voices from the Field: Leading Transformation in a VUCA World: A Progressive Vision for Brigantine Public School District 33
Glenn Robbins

Part II Go Where the Smart People Are—Learning from Others 41

3 Networks and Professional Organizations 43

4 Language Matters 51

Voices from the Field: My Journey of People-Centered Leadership as Superintendent 59
Zandra Jo Galván

Part III You Can Do It 65

5 We're Not Broke, We're Broken 67

6 Transformation: Flip the Mindset 81

Voices from the Field: Expanding Pathways to Success 91
Gladys I. Cruz

Part IV Change Faster—Embrace Your Context—Revolutionary Change 101

7 Bomb Threats and Social Media 103

8 Artificial Intelligence and Innovation 115

Voices from the Field: The Student's Bill of Rights 133
Jeff Dillon

Conclusion 139

Appendix A: Interviews from the Pandemic Era—Use Case for Generative AI and Leadership 145
Appendix B : AI in Education: Opportunities and Challenges 166
Appendix C: Generative Artificial Intelligence Tools Used Throughout This Book and NSSD 112 Board Policy Information 169
References 171
About the Contributors 175
About the Authors 177

Preface

A leader takes people where they want to go. A great leader takes people where they don't necessarily want to go, but ought to be.
—*Rosalynn Carter, former first lady of the United States*

Johannes Gutenberg was born in 1395 in Germany. His family worked in goldsmithing and gem cutting. As an adult, he was looking for ways to make money and pay off his personal debts. If you play word association with someone and say the name Gutenberg, most people will know he's the guy who invented the printing press. (Either that, or they will mention one of the co-leads in *Three Men and a Baby*.)

Prior to Johannes Gutenberg, all books that existed were hand-copied. That meant that books were available primarily to the social elites and the clergy. Gutenberg had an idea to create a machine with movable blocks of letters that could produce texts. He didn't know it at the time, but Johannes Gutenberg was "leading for tomorrow's schools today"—in 1440. His invention would revolutionize the availability of information for the masses and, in turn, would revolutionize the ability to provide widespread education.

His invention was not without difficulties and challenges. He experimented with a variety of materials and inks before he found a combination that would transfer well to paper consistently. He took on loans from investors, and when he was originally unable to produce a final product, he was sued by the investors who were trying to recapture their investments. Until the advent of the internet, his work defined the universal availability of knowledge to the broader masses. None of us needs to be the next Johannes Gutenberg, but we all have the responsibility and calling to make decisions today that will impact our students' success in their future world.

In *Leading for Tomorrow's Schools Today,* two "in-the-seat" superintendents, reflecting on more than thirty years combined as superintendents and nearly sixty years combined in education illustrate how innovative practices and challenging the process can and do lead to sustained change. To be clear, we are telling the stories of our people. We may have created the conditions, nudged, or supported the change process, but the credit goes where it is due: our faculty, staff, students, communities, and Boards of Education.

The insights in this book can also be applied to leadership and management in other sectors; the principles are not limited to education. Like Carter's quote, we attempt to take people where they ought to go—that's *great* leadership (and that is likely why you are reading this book right now).

The overall focus of the book is to help support conditions for growth, learning, success, and possibility. One way to do this is to learn from examples. That's what we hope to provide in the chapters ahead. Over the years, we have personally learned from research, observation, site visits, and local stories, and we're proud to share and illustrate the how and the what involved in educational change. The future workforce depends on us to create conditions that will allow for a brighter future for the next generation. More importantly, our kids depend on us to see around the corner and prepare them for a world that has yet to exist.

There are many models and approaches to change. We will be using the change model created by Virginia Satir as a consistent thread throughout each chapter. In an effort to contextualize change and to support how this can be replicated by our readers, we start with an introduction to that particular model. The Satir Change Model is a valuable tool for understanding and facilitating personal and organizational change. It consists of five stages:

- Current Status Quo;
- Introduction of a Foreign Element;
- Chaos (Transforming Ideas);
- Integration & Practice;
- New Status Quo.

See Figure P.1 for an illustration of the stages of change reflected in the Satir Model.

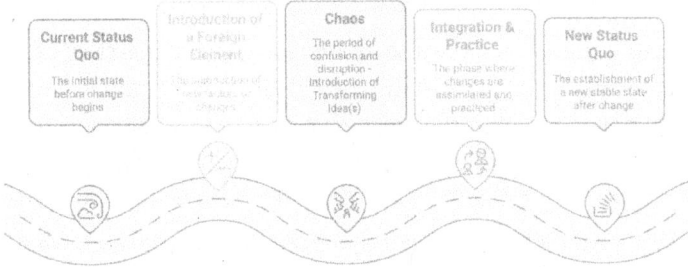

Figure P.1 Satir Change Model. Illustration by Michael Lubelfeld.

This model helps individuals and organizations navigate change by addressing emotional and psychological aspects. Throughout the book, we will apply the change management and leadership process to this long-standing model for clarity and continuity.

Another tip of the hat to leading for tomorrow's schools today comes in the form of the "craze" around generative artificial intelligence. The use of generative artificial intelligence models (Gen AI) has expanded "exponentially" since November 2023 with OpenAI's release of ChatGPT. Many Gen AI models have impacted various industries, including education.

One recurring theme you'll see is the reality that focusing on the future, while leading in the present, is essential for successful change leaders and community leaders. An illustration of this comes in the form of generative artificial intelligence tools. We believe that leaders who understand how and when to use Gen AI will far surpass those who resist, reject, or ignore this accelerator.

Therefore, in writing of this book, we will illustrate Gen AI use cases. One of these tools is from a partnership between the Association for Supervision & Curriculum Development (ASCD) and the International Society for Technology in Education (ISTE), the ASCD-ISTE "STRETCH" AI Chatbot.

In an effort to illustrate the power of AI in explaining complex concepts like the Satir Change Model, we used STRETCH AI for reference.

Stretch AI is a test coach in a "walled garden" approach that is for educators. We share the response to the prompt, *Virginia Satir has a model of change, can you explain it?* Let's pair that artificial intelligence response with what we know about Johannes Gutenberg:

1. *Late Status Quo:* The first stage represents the initial state or the status quo. At this stage, individuals or organizations may experience a sense of stability, but there are underlying issues or dissatisfaction that may lead to the recognition of the need for change.

    In the early 1400s, all texts were hand-copied and available only to the social elites and the clergy. There was no legitimate way to make information and education available to the masses.

2. *Foreign Element:* In this stage, a new idea, challenge, or external factor (the foreign element) is introduced. This could be a new perspective, a problem, or an opportunity that disrupts the status quo and prompts the need for change.

    Johannes Gutenberg needed to make some money and used his knowledge of goldsmithing and gem cutting to develop and refine an idea for the printing press. His investors lost patience with him and presented legal challenges in addition to his mechanical challenges.

3. *Chaos:* The introduction of the foreign element can lead to a period of chaos or confusion as individuals or organizations grapple with the impact of the change. This stage is characterized by uncertainty and a sense of disorganization.

    The introduction of the printing press considerably changed the world. Information was quickly becoming more available to the masses. This created dissonance and challenges to existing power structures. Education could now be available to a wider spectrum of people, and that wasn't accepted by all people.

4. *Integration:* As individuals or organizations begin to make sense of the change and its implications, they move toward integration. This involves exploring new possibilities, adapting to the change, and finding ways to incorporate the foreign element into the existing system.

    Over time, Gutenberg's invention became the norm throughout the world. It makes you wonder if there were ever concerns about taking away the jobs of the people who hand-copied texts. That's certainly what we are hearing today about the impacts of artificial intelligence.

5. *New Status Quo:* The final stage represents the establishment of a new status quo. At this stage, individuals or organizations have successfully integrated the change, and a new sense of stability and equilibrium is achieved. This new state may continue until the introduction of another foreign element, initiating the cycle once again.

Throughout our lives, we always knew that the daily newspapers would be printed and delivered to our front porches. We've always known that we can go to a bookstore or a website and find a copy of the latest book. This new status quo maps all the way back to the work of Johannes Gutenberg.

The Satir Change Model emphasizes the emotional and psychological aspects of change, acknowledging the challenges and opportunities that come with transitions. It provides a framework for understanding the process of change and the emotional responses that accompany it.

When explaining the Satir Change Model, it's important to highlight the dynamic nature of change and the need for individuals and organizations to navigate the stages of change with empathy, understanding, and resilience.

Throughout the book, we'll continue to share real examples illustrating how various chatbots (in 2024 at the time of the writing) are useful in sourcing, researching, aiding, supporting, and accelerating information and access.

We strongly emphasize the need for original thought and authorship, and we acknowledge the power of large language models to enhance and add efficiency to communication. We share multiple examples of Gen AI and acknowledge the limitations and biases. We recommend exploration of options like LatimerAI and others to round out the potential limitations of some models. Our point and purpose in applying Gen AI to this book is in part to illustrate courageous, brave, vulnerable, bold, and humble leadership approaches. We (and you) cannot do this alone. We need help, support, guidance, and assistance in all facets of life, including leadership. We provide the conditions, but leadership and change come from the whole organization.

The Satir Model essentially shows that when a change is introduced, the chaos/disequilibrium grows over time until a transformational event takes place and the integration & practice of the change is accepted and a new status quo is established. Note, though, that there is always some dissonance and disequilibrium—see the "squiggly lines" that show, even during "status quo"—there is some unease. If you don't believe us, look at the results of every climate and culture survey ever given in an organization. Dissonance, at some level, is a constant.

Change models are crucial for effective leadership. Throughout the book, we'll emphasize the need for leaders to unlearn. We argue that in order to prepare for tomorrow, much of what leaders have learned must be reconsidered and unlearned. We advocate for leading today with an eye toward creating a better future for our nation's children.

Finally, for the case study examples we share, we also apply our own framework reflected by the acronym CHANGE. See Figure P.2 for a graphic example of this.

By applying the CHANGE Leadership framework to past, present, and future leadership actions, transformative change can become the norm as we lead for tomorrow's schools today. We'll revisit this throughout the book, and we'll apply case studies shared through the Satir Model and our CHANGE

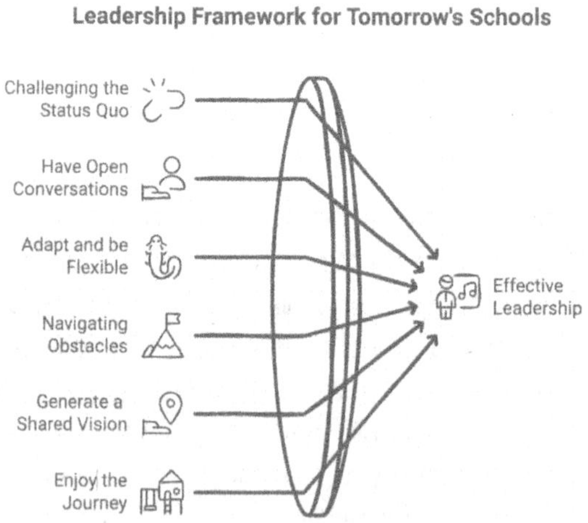

Leadership Framework for Tomorrow's Schools

- Challenging the Status Quo
- Have Open Conversations
- Adapt and be Flexible
- Navigating Obstacles
- Generate a Shared Vision
- Enjoy the Journey

→ Effective Leadership

Figure P.2 CHANGE leadership framework. © Lubelfeld & Polyak.

Leadership Framework Model. As depicted in Figure P.2, the CHANGE Leadership Framework means,

- C—Challenge the status quo,
- H—Have open conversations,
- A—Adapt and be flexible,
- N—Navigate obstacles,
- G—Generate a shared vision,
- E—Enjoy the journey

John O'Leary, in his book *In Awe*, states:

> How often do you have the brakes on in your life?
> In my experience, when we get stuck doing things the same way we've always done them, we have the brakes on.
> When we accept that the status quo is as good as it's gonna get; when we listen to the voices that say in can't be done, including our own; when we see only discord and difficulty, and decide not to even try; when we believe that things are impossible; it means the brakes are holding us back. (45)

Let's release those brakes! Let's Lead for Tomorrow's Schools Today!

Foreword

by Thomas C. Murray

If you're holding this book, chances are you already know that today's educational landscape is a bit like steering a ship through unpredictable waters—full of waves, shifting currents, and the occasional *"Why didn't we see that coming?"* storm. But here's the good news: *Leading for Tomorrow's Schools Today* doesn't just hand you the wheel and hope for the best. Instead, it offers a map and the needed tools, combined with real-world insights, to help you navigate the complexities of leading in a world where the horizon always seems to be shifting.

Today, the stakes for school and district leaders have never been higher. We aren't just educating learners for today's world; we're preparing *future-ready learners* to thrive in a world that is rapidly changing. But don't worry; you're not in this alone. In the work you are about to read, authors Michael Lubelfeld and Nick Polyak, with their decades of combined leadership experience, have equipped themselves with the wisdom (and scars) to help you navigate today's issues through a comprehensive leadership framework that puts trust, empathy, and innovation at the center of everything. They remind us that leadership is about cultivating a growth mindset, not just for our learners but for ourselves and our entire educational community.

But let's be clear: this book isn't about sitting around waiting for change to happen. It's about rolling up your sleeves and leading from the front, as it's not a passive role. It requires the active cultivation of a vision that transcends current challenges and anticipates the needs of the future. It means setting the tone, creating a culture of trust, and having the courage to make the needed decisions, even when they're unpopular. If we want today's modern learners to have opportunities and thrive in tomorrow's workforce, then we need to start now—because tomorrow isn't waiting for us to catch up.

As the authors eloquently share, creating a culture of trust is foundational to success in this work. Trust is the bedrock upon which all successful and sustainable change is built. Without it, even the most well-intentioned initiatives will falter. The authors show how trust is not merely a concept but a practice that must be embedded in every decision, every interaction, and every policy. This culture of trust fosters an environment where innovation can thrive, where educators feel empowered to try new things and grow, and where learners are encouraged to take risks and fail forward as they navigate personal and authentic learning experiences.

At the core of *Leading for Tomorrow's Schools Today* is the reminder that leadership is both an art and a science. It's about making calculated and intentional choices while staying nimble enough to pivot when things inevitably change. Overcoming the mentality of *"that's the way we've always done it"* is perhaps one of the most significant challenges facing today's educators. This book is a clarion call to all who lead in education to break free from the constraints of tradition and embrace a future-focused approach, as our kids deserve nothing less.

One of the most compelling aspects of this book is its unflinching examination of the need for leaders to make challenging decisions in the best interest of our learners, and Lubelfeld and Polyak are not afraid to get real about the challenges in doing so. Leadership, at its core, is about making tough choices—choices that may not always be popular but are necessary for the long-term success of learners. The stories and case studies intentionally shared in this book highlight the importance of prioritizing learners' needs above all else, even when it means facing resistance or making sacrifices. The future we're preparing them for demands nothing less.

As you turn these pages, prepare to think beyond the walls of your school or district and into the future we are all building. *Leading for Tomorrow's Schools Today* is more than a guide; it's a call to action. The future of education isn't a distant concept—it's happening right now.

So, grab your life jacket for the challenging times and prepare to lead—right now. The future—and our learners—are waiting.

Acknowledgments

Nick and Mike

We want to thank the reviewers and endorsers of our book; the professional collegiality is meaningful, and we are so grateful to you for your time, energy, wisdom, and support! We thank Tom, Glenn, Zandra, Gladys, and Jeff for joining our call to action and sharing their incredible thoughts in the book, in the foreword, and the voices from the field vignettes after each section. We thank our publisher, Bloomsbury Academic, for support and encouragement. Carrie and Jasmine, thank you for your encouragement and patience. We extend a special thank you to Eileen M. Strider, president of The Virginia Satir Global Network, for her exceptional support, advice, and grounding in the Satir Change Process.

We thank the AASA for co-publishing and supporting our leadership, growth, and development, and for helping us lead for tomorrow's schools every day. Thank you to Brian and Anthony for taking the time to offer us critical feedback and profound guidance.

Mike

I want to thank the teachers with whom I work and from whom I learn each and every day. I want to thank the teachers with whom I taught side by side for so many years. I want to thank the Board of Education in North Shore School District 112 for their support of our "inspire, innovate, engage" motto each day. I want to thank the many partners of District 112 with whom I have worked, learned, grown, and led. To the members of the Leadership Team in District 112—Thank you—from the bottom of my heart, thank you for leading with passion, purpose, power, and energy for our many years together! Monica, I've left the campfire in a better place than when I found it—success and happiness to you!!

I want to dedicate this book to my wife Stephanie, my daughter Maya (a teacher in training), and to my son Justin. They are my teachers each and every day! For every success I have had in my career, I want to thank James R. Newlin, Jr.—Jim—you were, are, and will always be a hero to me.

Nick

I have the best job in the world. Our teachers and support staff members spend thirty to forty (and sometimes even more) years of their lives serving our students and community. Our administrative team laughs together while they lead together. Our Board of Education trusts us and gives us the latitude to do what's best for the kids every day. I feel so honored to be the superintendent of this amazing school district. And I'm honored to share some of their stories in this book. I dedicate these pages to all of them.

Introduction

Leading for Tomorrow's Schools Today is designed as a call to action for all stakeholders in the educational ecosystem—educators, policymakers, school board members, and community leaders. This is not just a book to read but a manifesto to act upon. We aim to catalyze a movement of educational reform that respects the past but is resolutely focused on the future.

In *Leading for Tomorrow's Schools Today*, we empower current and future educational leaders with a transformative framework for action. This book synthesizes our decades of leadership experiences across school systems nationally and internationally, guiding you through proven strategies to actively forge a bright future for education.

Reflecting on the wisdom of John Adams, who once said, "No man is entirely free from weakness and imperfection in this life," we recognize that educational leadership is a journey of continual learning and adaptation. This book is crafted to illustrate how leaders can overcome the inherent challenges of their roles and implement lasting changes that profoundly impact educational outcomes.

Our body of work and observations of effective leadership around the nation and world encourage you to challenge the status quo, embrace growth, and foster environments that cultivate future-ready learners rather than replicating past inefficiencies. Each chapter is structured to offer reflection questions and case studies, alongside leadership blueprints modeled on the Satir Change Model described in the Preface, to facilitate both introspection and practical application. To guide our journey, we rely on proven leadership frameworks that have consistently delivered results across various contexts. We introduce our own leadership framework, CHANGE, throughout each chapter.

There is an urgency for change, especially in education. Consistent with Fullan and Quinn in their 2024 book *The Drivers: Transforming Learning for Students, Schools, and Systems*, we believe there is a need for deep learning and deep change. Fullan and Quinn share the following quote which conceptually is present throughout this book:

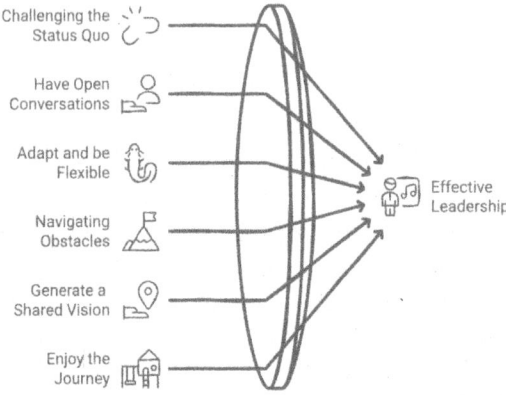

Figure I.1 CHANGE Leadership Framework. *Source:* Mike Lubelfeld and Nick Polyak.

> *When the status quo no longer works, an alternative is needed. The exciting finding is that an increasing number of schools and systems, including students, teachers, leaders, and communities are strongly attracted to what we call Deep Learning. . . . There is a growing recognition worldwide that a transformative change is needed. (112)*

As we write this book, we're on a mission to take the past eight years since our first book, with three additional books and a host of leadership challenges and successes in between, to ideate how, together, we can Lead for Tomorrow's Schools—Today! We review and learn from leaders like Fullan, Quinn, O'Leary, and many others as we share a compelling vision for leadership and change.

In each chapter of this book, we'll share commentary and examples broadly about challenging the process. Many write that "That's the Way We Always Do it" is the greatest challenge and enemy to change. We agree, and we thrive when we can help leaders implement change and build coalitions of the willing to make things better for all they serve. Each chapter has reflection questions at the start and near the end. Reader engagement and reflection are essential as guiding thinking, leading, and transformational change.

The book is organized into four parts: Part I: Leadership Is Change, Part II: Go Where the Smart People Are—Learning from Others, Part III: You Can Do It, and Part IV: Change Faster—Embrace Your Context—Revolutionary

Change. Each part has two chapters and concludes with a voice from the field (commentary from our friends and colleagues across the country).

We focus on cultivating the garden, or creating the proper conditions for change, in Chapter 1. Then, in Chapter 2, we move into the selection of staff. In Chapter 3, we explore professional networks and opportunities to grow from beyond your local lens. In Chapter 4, we address how transformational change in a theater department impacts the entire school and community and lasts for years. In Chapter 5, we explore a district in turmoil and how it emerged. In Chapter 6, we share new ways to organize a high school experience. In Chapter 7, we explore the impacts of social media usage and restrictions. And Chapter 8 focuses on artificial intelligence and innovation.

The primary goal of this book is to empower educators and leaders to foster environments that enhance growth, learning, and success. Drawing from extensive research, observations, site visits, and local stories, we provide actionable insights into effective change and growth planning.

The impacts of the Covid-19 global pandemic are still within reach, so in Appendix A we share leadership lessons, philosophical approaches, and communication addressing the impacts and lessons learned from that multi-year experience. We share illustrations of restored community faith, financial success, and long-term sustainability for a school district.

Every student's experience in their current grade is unique and irreplaceable. Therefore, it is essential that we consistently create conditions that promote growth and achievement, ensuring every interaction contributes to their future success. We draw on our experiences as superintendents and owe a debt of gratitude to the thousands of students, teachers, educational staff members, board of education members, fellow administrators, and colleagues around the world for inspiration!

As context for our case studies, we offer overviews of each of our current school districts (drawn from ChatGPT 4-o). This is both for the context of where we currently work and serves as an example of the utility of generative artificial intelligence.

The book is for all educators, school and district leaders, board members, policymakers, association leaders, and the general public. *Leading for Tomorrow's Schools Today* provides that essential guide. Don't just dream of change; achieve it. This playbook shows you how. The future of our nation rests within the imagination of today's school leaders. As parents, the success of the future for our own children and future grandchildren compels us to act and share our daring change processes and tips with others.

Overview of North Shore School District 112 (Highland Park, IL)

North Shore School District 112 (NSSD112), located in the diverse and vibrant communities of Highland Park and Highwood, Illinois, is committed to delivering innovative and equitable education for its students. Serving over 3,700 pre-kindergarten through eighth-grade students across multiple schools, NSSD112 is known for its dual-language programs, robust arts and music initiatives, and strong focus on academic excellence. The district embraces a mission of creating inclusive learning environments that foster intellectual curiosity, critical thinking, and social-emotional growth. Central to NSSD112's strategic vision is its commitment to long-range facilities planning, which has driven substantial modernization efforts through partnerships with firms like Wight & Company. As a leader in forward-thinking educational practices, the district integrates cutting-edge technology and personalized learning approaches to meet the needs of a diverse student body, all while maintaining strong community engagement and high standards of operational transparency.

With a rich history of success in developing students for future readiness, NSSD112 has a strong emphasis on leadership development at every level, from students to staff. Mike Lubelfeld's leadership, supported by a dedicated team, has fostered a culture of continuous improvement, using both traditional frameworks and generative artificial intelligence to enhance educational outcomes. The district's global service-learning programs, particularly its annual student trips to the Dominican Republic, exemplify its commitment to cultivating globally aware, socially conscious citizens who are prepared to thrive in an interconnected world.

Overview of Leyden High School District 212 (Franklin Park, IL)

Leyden High School District 212, located in Franklin Park, Illinois, is a dynamic and progressive school district that serves the suburban communities of Franklin Park, Schiller Park, Rosemont, River Grove, Northlake, Melrose Park, and unincorporated Leyden Township. Comprising East and West Leyden High Schools, District 212 serves a richly diverse student body of approximately 3,500 students. Leyden is renowned for its forward-thinking approach to education, placing an emphasis on personalized learning, equity, and technology integration. As a national leader in 1:1 technology programs, Leyden High School District was one of the first three in the country to provide every student with a Chromebook, exemplifying its commitment to equipping students with the tools they need to succeed in a rapidly evolving world.

Under the visionary leadership of Superintendent Nick Polyak, Leyden has implemented several key initiatives focused on expanding college and career readiness, social-emotional support, and real-world learning experiences. The district prides itself on fostering a culture of innovation and collaboration, where educators and students work together to break down traditional educational silos and create meaningful, personalized pathways to success. Leyden's emphasis on career and technical education (CTE) programs, along with its growing partnerships with local industries, allows students to graduate not only with academic knowledge but also with practical skills and certifications that position them for success in post-secondary education and the workforce. The district's innovative spirit and dedication to meeting the unique needs of each student make it a model of twenty-first-century education.

Join us on this crucial journey to redefine educational standards. *Leading for Tomorrow's Schools Today* offers practical advice, compelling case studies, and a solid theoretical framework, equipping you to profoundly impact student lives and society at large. Let's collaborate to establish the foundations today that will ensure the excellence of tomorrow's schools.

Part I
Leadership Is Change

1 Cultivating Change

A leader must also tend his garden; he, too, plants seeds, and then watches, cultivates, and harvests the results. Like the gardener, a leader must take responsibility for what he cultivates; he must mind his work..., preserve what can be preserved, and eliminate what cannot succeed.

—*Nelson Mandela*

With respect to Leading for Tomorrow's Schools Today as a concept, or as a mindset, it can be argued that much of the workforce of yesterday is, well, *irrelevant*. The twenty-first century is a quarter over. It's time to focus our efforts on the creation of what the twenty-second century will need from our students. It's imperative that leaders create conditions where what's working can be cultivated and what's not working can be "weeded and pruned."

With that in mind, our imperative becomes clear: we must lead today's schools to prepare for tomorrow's workforce. Our students depend on us to create conditions that foster their growth, achievement, and future readiness. So too, do our teachers and administrators.

In this first chapter, we start with the premise that we need to cultivate change in the same way a gardener cultivates their garden. Remove "things" that neither work nor contribute to student success as we add or amend to the list of things that do contribute in positive ways. Focus on the who, what, when, why, and how—remembering your why throughout. Prune and weed so that growth can occur without obstacles.

In each chapter of the book, we ask that you take some time to reflect. We have questions for your own review, growth, and development. Some people like to keep a journal as they read; we encourage you to do so if that will aid your reflections. As you read Chapter 1, please consider the following reflection questions,

- What is an example of something you've stopped doing in order to "cultivate change" and make room for new and different work?
- Who do you know that is good at identifying practices that are outdated or ineffective? What can you learn from that person?

- How do you balance the change sought with the capacity for the organization to change?
- In what ways do you see yourself as a gardener, like the Mandela quote at the start of the chapter?

Generally speaking, people often view change as another thing they have to do. Our youth deserve unprecedented leadership. They deserve equitable access to the best educational opportunities. They deserve, and society deserves, for their education to be maximized.

Schools are among the most impactful places in the lives of our students, but if our educators are overwhelmed by change, we cannot realize that mission. That said, change is often viewed as loss, and there is typically resistance to change.

In 2016, Douglas Reeves urged leaders to "weed [their] educational garden" and focus their time only on projects that directly support their identified purpose. In 2017, our book *The Unlearning Leader* explored the concept of "unlearning"—the deliberate process of letting go of outdated facts and theories to embrace new, more relevant information. This book builds on that foundation, emphasizing the urgency of leadership that fosters immediate and effective change.

> *Our youth (and we) live in a world of exponential growth, change, technology, input, stimuli, etc. We must impact our schools today so that we can have the best tomorrow possible. We do not need to wait—we cannot wait! While we're really good at learning things, in general, it's not so easy for us to unlearn, relearn, and change.*

In our 2021 book, *The Unfinished Leader: A School Leadership Framework for Growth & Development*, we wrote about the difficulties involved with change:

> *Let's start off by acknowledging why change is so hard. Change is incredibly hard for four reasons. First, change represents loss. Second, our brain desires certainty and is risk-averse and change is anything but. Next, leading change is expensive. It creates a large emotional toll and is costly to the political capital you have worked so hard to earn. Lastly, in order to lead change, you must have the talent or skill to see things for better than they currently are. (170)*

So the change leader, the leader who is actually leading for tomorrow's schools today, must be equipped with the knowledge that even removing something that is no longer improving the organization will cause challenges as you try to remove it.

Our hope for you is that we are starting off a journey of reflection, planning, learning, and leading. We start with a contemporary example of "stopping" that is going around the nation as we prepare this manuscript: cell phone bans and prohibitions in schools. While we neither advocate for nor oppose this particular topic, we are identifying it as this appears to be a nationwide trend at the time of our writing. In each chapter of the book, we share a case study from the profession or from our own practice, and we run the case study through two change models. We're using the Satir Model of Change as we explained earlier in the Preface, and we're also going to use our own CHANGE model.

For a host of reasons, schools and school districts around the United States are banning (or restricting) the use of cellular phones/devices as they have become a large distraction and a contributor to mental health issues among our nation's youth. Some schools are locking the devices up into pouches, others require them to be off and secure in lockers, and others have strong punishments for rule violations.

The weeding of the garden, or cultivating for change, for purposes of our analysis, is the removal of non-district technology devices and personal student communication devices from classrooms and schools during the day. Let's look at this idea through the lenses of the Satir Model of Change:

- *Current Status Quo:* Since 2007, with the inception of the iPhone from Apple, cellular devices took the world by storm, and many technology initiatives in schools relied on BYOD (or bring your own device) for many years.
- *Foreign Element:* Before we knew it, cell phones became an extension of our bodies and a fixture in our lives. With the advent of social media platforms, cyberbullying became a reality and the US Surgeon General declared a Mental Health Crisis for our Nation's Youth in 2021.
- *Chaos:* Leadership changes and failed initiatives created turmoil, students wanted their phones, teachers did not want to be enforcers, and there were mixed views of the actual negative impact of cellular technology. Was it a scapegoat for other societal ills? How do you

reverse decades of free usage? There are conflicting views and difficult decisions to make.

- *Integration:* As we are writing this, there is a new school year and a host of districts around the nation "banning" the devices. We are in the middle of integration now and we'll see how this goes and grows into the new normal of school operations.
- *New Status Quo:* This is yet to be seen, of course, as this is a real change in process. However, the early reports are that student engagement is increasing. Also, this new status quo (similar to former realities), features students talking to one another during downtime rather than turning to their phones.

As educational leaders, we have all lived through the digital revolution. We've navigated the arrival of Chromebooks, laptops, tablets, and more that have redefined the way we "do" teaching and learning. We have provided devices, allowed students to bring their own devices, and we have supplied internet hot spots. We have switched to virtual textbooks, collaborative online documents, and E-Learning Days. We've even made it through prolonged virtual learning during a global pandemic.

It's strange and nostalgic to take a moment to refresh and reset to list some recent technological advancements as reference to how "young" many technologies are, and how "modern" somethings that have become ubiquitous, were not always so. Some examples are shown in Figure 1.1, Major Technological Creations Timeline, 1995–2024.

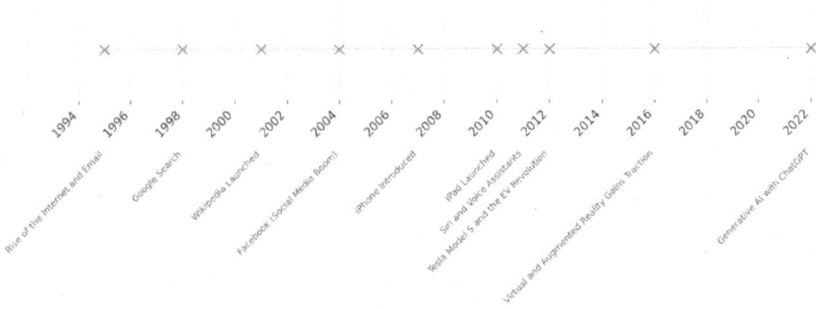

Figure 1.1 Major technological creations timeline, 1995–2024. Illustration by Michael Lubelfeld and Nick Polyak.

The current technological accelerator, generative artificial intelligence, or Gen AI, is prolific in society, and throughout this book. In consideration of leading for tomorrow's schools today, we identify, illustrate, and apply Gen AI as an example of forward-looking change, even when there is much yet to learn about this.

The 2024 book *Co-Intelligence* by Ethan Mollick explores how generative AI systems, like GPT-4, can be harnessed as co-workers, co-teachers, and coaches to enhance human capabilities. We argue that mastering collaboration with AI is essential for navigating the future of work and learning.

Throughout all of this technological change, with the views and approaches to cellular devices in the schools, one of the common denominators has been a desire for a modicum of protection. Content filters and cybersecurity tools are able to keep many of the bad things away. There are programs that can monitor the safety and well-being of our students. In schools, generally, we can regulate accessibility to social media sites and much more via our Wi-Fi networks and firewalls. During this transformation, we have often considered cell phones in the same thoughts with open access to technology. However, there is one significant difference—cellular wide open access.

Operating on the cellular network, cell phones live outside most, if not all, of the district's protections. They buzz, ding, and vibrate as they connect students 24/7 to their various social media accounts. Their cell phones are an amazing resource while also creating the possibility for constant distraction. Rather than adding education benefits, they often create less engagement in the classroom, creating a non-stop disciplinary issue between students, teachers, families, and administrators.

Let's look at how this nationwide restriction effort on cellular devices can be analyzed through utilization of our CHANGE Leadership Framework:

- *C—Challenge the Status Quo:* Cellular devices have been present in schools as soon as they were available, they defined early 1:1 technology initiatives in the 2000s and 2010s. They were illustrative of "technology-friendly schools" and now we're challenging that status quo and seeking change through weeding the garden.
- *H—Have Open Conversations:* There are many stakeholders involved with this issue. You will need to speak with students and families about changes to how you handle those $1,000+ devices in their pockets and on their wrists. You should speak openly with your

teachers, technology staff, and mental health professionals as you make decisions on this topic.

- *A—Adapt and Be Flexible:* School districts are addressing cell phones by a variety of strategies. They are asking students to leave phones at home, leave them in lockers, place them in pouches on the wall, place them in lockable pouches, and more. Whatever the strategy, schools are trying new and different things that involve purchases and often changes to what's available in every classroom.

- *N—Navigate Obstacles:* Aside from the costs associated with this change, you can anticipate pushback from some students and parents. In an era where the possibility of school violence unfortunately exists, many parents want the security of knowing they can reach their children at all times. Students may share vocal opposition or actively find ways to circumvent your efforts. They are VERY creative. Finally, you need to navigate the financial liability of what might happen with damaged or stolen phones when the school district is removing them from the students. What about the obstacle of the child who needs the social connection via the cellular device as part of a medical plan, or an individualized education plan? What about personalized learning or diabetes monitoring?

- *G—Generate a Shared Vision:* Why are we making this change? In order for it to be successful, we need all stakeholders to understand the answer to that question. In this case, it is about increasing student engagement and academic outcomes by removing a universal distraction. When we are all grounded in that rationale, it makes our actions and conversations consistent and more meaningful.

- *E—Enjoy the Journey:* In this case, we can enjoy the journey by mirroring these expectations as much as possible for the adults who share these spaces with students. If we want kids to put away their phones, engage in learning, and talk to one another, we should expect the same of ourselves. By simply modeling the way, we can actually experience the same benefits of this change.

Now is a great time to get your journal, or reflective space, to consider the following reflection questions again. Have your responses or reflections changed as a result of the chapter? Are you considering reading the book in chronological order or are you seeking specific content/topics?

- What is an example of something you've stopped doing in order to "cultivate change" and make room for new and different work?
- Who do you know that is good at identifying practices that are outdated or ineffective? What can you learn from that person?
- How do you balance the change sought with the capacity for the organization to change?
- In what ways do you see yourself as a gardener, like the Mandela quote at the start of the chapter?

As referenced, Gen AI is quite prolific at the time of this writing, and throughout the book including a chapter dedicated to the subject, we illustrate multiple use cases for these Gen AI tools.

For this chapter, we prompted Claude AI, a generative AI tool from Anthropic, the following: Claude, we are writing a book on leadership, the first chapter is entitled Cultivating Change, we're showing examples of use cases for generative AI, like you, can you please respond to this prompt: We are writing a book, the first chapter is called Cultivating Change, can you please speak to K–12 Education (the book is called Leading for Tomorrow's Schools Today) and offer guidance on how leaders can cultivate change as they lead for tomorrow's schools today.

This is the output from Claude AI:

> *For the chapter "Cultivating Change" in your book **Leading for Tomorrow's Schools Today**, here's some guidance on how K–12 education leaders can cultivate change as they prepare schools for the future:*
>
> **1.** *Embrace a growth mindset: Leaders should model and encourage a culture of continuous learning and adaptation. This mindset is crucial for navigating the rapidly changing educational landscape.*
>
> **2.** *Develop a compelling vision: Create and communicate a clear, inspiring vision of what tomorrow's schools could and should look like. This vision should align with emerging trends in education, technology, and society.*
>
> **3.** *Foster innovation: Encourage experimentation with new teaching methods, technologies, and curricula. Create safe spaces for teachers to take risks and learn from failures.*

4. *Prioritize digital literacy:* Ensure that both educators and students are equipped with the digital skills necessary for success in an increasingly technology-driven world.
5. *Emphasize twenty-first-century skills:* Focus on developing critical thinking, creativity, collaboration, and communication skills alongside traditional academic subjects.
6. *Personalize learning:* Leverage technology and data to create more individualized learning experiences that cater to each student's needs, interests, and pace.
7. *Build partnerships:* Collaborate with local businesses, community organizations, and higher education institutions to create real-world learning opportunities and ensure curriculum relevance.
8. *Invest in professional development:* Provide ongoing training and support for teachers to help them adapt to new pedagogies and technologies.
9. *Promote diversity and inclusion:* Ensure that educational practices and policies are equitable and inclusive, preparing students for a diverse, global society.
10. *Cultivate emotional intelligence:* Recognize the importance of social-emotional learning for both students and staff, particularly in times of change.
11. *Embrace flexibility:* Design learning environments and schedules that can adapt to changing needs and circumstances.
12. *Engage stakeholders:* Involve teachers, students, parents, and community members in the change process to build buy-in and gather diverse perspectives.
13. *Lead by example:* Demonstrate adaptability, resilience, and a willingness to learn from mistakes as you navigate the change process.
14. *Monitor and evaluate:* Regularly assess the impact of changes and be willing to adjust strategies based on evidence and feedback.
15. *Balance tradition and innovation:* While embracing change, also preserve valuable aspects of traditional education that remain relevant and effective.

When implementing these changes, it's crucial to:

- *Involve stakeholders in the decision-making process;*
- *Communicate clearly about why changes are being made;*
- *Provide support during transitions;*
- *Monitor the impact of changes and be willing to make further adjustments as needed.*

These strategies can help school leaders "cultivating change" by addressing issues proactively and fostering a thriving school environment. Often we hear about initiative fatigue from teachers, school leaders, and others when they are asked to start something new or add to their already crowded plates. The concept of weeding the garden allows leaders to take away that which is not working or is actually a distraction before adding something new or embarking on a new adventure.

(Ok—this is the humans writing again.) Effective school leadership requires ongoing evaluation and elimination of ineffective practices, policies, and programs to improve educational outcomes and operational efficiency. This process demands systematic evaluation, data-driven decision-making, willingness to change, a continuous improvement mindset, and stakeholder involvement. Leading for tomorrow's schools today requires throwing out the "TTWWADI"—That's The Way We Always Do It—mindset. It's time to embrace change and understand its impact.

2 Selection of Staff
Who, How, and How Long?

Great vision without great people is irrelevant.
— Jim Collins

According to the National Center for Education Statistics, 86 percent of US K–12 public schools reported challenges hiring teachers for the 2023–24 school year, with 83 percent reporting trouble hiring for non-teacher positions such as classroom aides, transportation staff, and mental health professionals. At the same time, Gallup reports that 39 percent of teachers feel "burned out" either always or very often.

Finally, EdWeek reports that 35 percent of teachers plan to leave the profession within the next two years. When you put these data points together, it's clear that we need to focus our efforts on the recruitment, selection, and retention of staff as a significant priority in every school and district across the country.

As we prepare for the future workforce and schools, it's clear that the workforce of yesterday is in danger of becoming no longer relevant. Leading for tomorrow's schools today requires us to act now. With the twenty-first century already a quarter over, it's time to focus on shaping the twenty-second century through our leadership efforts. We need the right people in the right roles to drive this transformation.

As you read this chapter, consider the reflective questions,

- In what ways does your organization approach recruitment, selection, and retention of staff?
- How can you align the efforts of your community, Board of Education, Administration, faculty, and staff when it comes to hiring?
- In what ways is your organization addressing the teacher/educator shortage?
- Considering the Big 5 Personality Theory (described in this chapter), how does it impact your view of your organization's selection process?

When considering future-focused leadership, we must constantly look at who is on the team before we ever look at where the team is going. We'll share practical advice on how to deliberately and intentionally use staff selection to lead for tomorrow's schools today. Jim Collins and others clearly compel the world that getting the right people in the right seats on the bus makes all the difference in the world.

In Nick's district, they were looking to tackle not only educator shortages but also issues of equity and representation. The graph below shows the ethnic background of both the students and the staff at Leyden Community High School District 212 as taken from the Illinois State Report Card for 2023 (see Table 2.1):

In 2022, the Leyden Board of Education approved an Equity and Justice Statement with six commitments. The second one stated that the district was committed to:

- Recruiting, hiring, and retaining a diverse staff that enhances the school community with regard to age, cultural background, physical abilities and disabilities, race, religion, sex, sexual identity, and gender identity.

The glaring data point in that graph is obviously that over 70 percent of the students identify as Hispanic, while less than 7 percent of the teaching staff identify as Hispanic. The district has historically recruited by attending

Table 2.1 Leyden High School Demographics

Demographics	Students (%)	Staff (%)
White	24	86.7
Black	1.5	1.3
Hispanic	70.6	6.8
Asian	2.7	1.7
American Indian	0.5	1.7
Pacific Islander	0	1.7
Two or More	0.7	0

job fairs, collaborating with local universities, posting on job sites, and doing the things that most school districts do. However, they came to the following conclusion: The only sure-fire way to hire more teachers that are reflective of their students is to hire more of their former students back as their teachers.

That realization led to the idea that they had to do everything they could to grow their own future teachers. With that, the district created an education pathway. In the classrooms, students learn how to be teachers, and they earn industry-recognized credentials. Students interested in early childhood or elementary education earn their Early Childhood Level 1 Credential while working in the district-run community preschool program.

Students interested in secondary education have opportunities to job shadow and teach in local partner school districts. They are often paired with teachers who are Leyden alumni. Through this mentorship, real-life teaching experiences, and community college dual credit, students learn about teaching by actually teaching.

As students complete these education pathways, they are invited to an Educator Signing Day. At this special ceremony, those students hear a keynote address from the current State Teacher of the Year or other educational dignitary. They are celebrated for their accomplishments and commitment to the field of education, and each student signs a letter of intent to become a teacher. This celebratory event is capped off when each student who successfully completes their education receives the district's Golden Ticket.

This "Willy Wonka" style Golden Ticket is meant to be posted in their college dorm rooms. It serves as a visual reminder that they are guaranteed an interview for a teaching job upon college graduation at Leyden or at any of their seven elementary feeder school districts. If they are hired to teach back at the Leyden High Schools, they will receive a $5,000 signing bonus. By offering this special access, Leyden aims to align their teaching population more closely with their student demographics. Rather than relying on hope or effort, they have developed an intentional and deliberate leadership model to achieve this goal (Figure 2.1).

Figure 2.1 Golden Ticket image. Illustration by Nick Polyak.

Taken from the Leyden Community High School District 212 website:

The mission of Leyden High School District 212 is to Educate, Enrich, and Empower our Students and Communities. The Board of Education at Leyden is committed to recruiting, hiring, and retaining a diverse staff that enhances the school community in regard to age, cultural background, physical abilities and disabilities, race, religion, sex, sexual identity, and gender identity.

Nationally, almost 60% of teachers are teaching within 20 miles of where they attended high school, but we want to make that even closer to home. Leyden District 212 is excited to announce our Golden Ticket initiative. We want successful Leyden graduates like you to come back home and teach at the Leyden High Schools or the elementary where you attended. We want passionate future educators like you to inspire the next generation of Leyden students.

As a Leyden graduate, you are guaranteed an interview for a teaching position at Leyden or the elementary district you graduated from. Leyden specifically is offering a $5,000 signing bonus if you are hired to teach full-time at one of the Leyden High Schools.

After being part of the #leydenpride family, we are aware that you know our community well and can connect with our students. We want to do everything we can to encourage teaching as a career path for our best and brightest. Come back home and help keep the Leyden community strong for the next generations of Eagles!

Applying the Leyden case study to the CHANGE process,

- *C—Challenge the Status Quo:* There is a difference between having 70 percent Hispanic students and 7 percent Hispanic teachers. Leyden challenged the status quo and decided to act and lead in new, transformative ways with the Golden Ticket program. In its first three years, six Leyden alumni have earned the $5,000 signing bonus!
- *H—Have Open Conversations:* Often it's difficult to have honest, open conversations about race, ethnicity, equity, and representation. Leyden leadership demonstrated courage, honesty, honor, and open conversation about ways in which they could address the representation gap between students and teachers in their district.
- *A—Adapt and Be Flexible:* Offering a cash signing bonus and guaranteeing interviews in eight school districts (Leyden plus its seven partner elementary school districts) exemplifies flexibility. This adaptive leadership approach aims to increase representation by inviting graduates to return and teach in their community.
- *N—Navigate Obstacles:* In implementing the Golden Ticket, the district needed to overcome a variety of concerns. There were existing employees who were alumni who did not receive this benefit. This benefit was given to teaching staff but not to support staff. Finally, they needed to overcome union and school board concerns about equitable treatment of staff. Ultimately, the overall goals of representation, and bringing more alumni back home were able to overcome any obstacles.
- *G—Generate a Shared Vision:* The shared vision of guaranteed interviews, supported by seven elementary school districts feeding into Leyden High Schools, underscores the collective commitment to the Golden Ticket initiative.
- *E—Enjoy the Journey:* Nick enjoys visiting the Golden Ticket $5,000 recipients on their first day in the classroom. Presenting that check and explaining that they have come back home, in front of their new students, is a highlight at the start of every school year now.

To some in human resources (HR), interviews or selection of staff is analogous to shooting craps in Las Vegas . . . roll the dice and hope for the best. That approach is flawed and is not designed to yield effective results nor will it sustain excellence in any organization. In this section, we'll share an illustration of successful evidence-based, disciplined approaches found in practice, that also embody Collins' quote we started the chapter with, *Great vision without great people is irrelevant.*

Over the past twelve years, in Mike's direct experience over two school districts, his systems implemented and applied evidence-based structured selection processes. We first wrote about this in our 2017 book, *The Unlearning Leader*, where we focused on the Deerfield Public Schools in suburban Chicago.

Applying the Satir Model of Change to the selection of staff process, we look to when Mike took the helm in Deerfield, IL as superintendent (2013). Mike's team made a significant change to the selection of staff. The results were positive, and to date, the processes are still in place there.

- *Current Status Quo:* The Deerfield Public Schools had leaders trained in structured selection but the organization lacked discipline and focus and it was "use if you want to" versus use because that is our way regarding selection of staff with evidence-based practices.
- *Foreign Element:* Some principals simply did not believe the research, evidence, or power of the protocols. They did not want to invest so much time and rigid disciplined energy toward the front-end of selection of staff.
- *Chaos:* The new superintendent and team were resolute and quite clear—there was no option to choose your own adventure anymore with the selection of staff. All leaders were retrained, there was a recommitment and a reeducation.
- *Integration:* Over a short period of time, the requirements for the selection of staff, teacher hiring, and staff hiring, became clear and understood. Even the loudest resistors came around as there was no option to fake it and the organization benefited from clear, consistent, coherent, and proven structures for selection of staff.
- *New Status Quo:* The selection of staff process has sustained three superintendent changes and more than a decade of implementation. It is the new and sustained normal.

Recently, Humanex Ventures' (a human capital consulting group) CEO and president Brad Black published a book entitled *Talent, Teams, & Culture* (2024).

In his book, elements of this structured, evidence-based, research-focused selection process are also outlined and explained. Basically, in order to be selected for a position (any position of employment) in the district where a structured process is used, an applicant must follow a number of disciplined and consistent steps yielding data for the organization at every stage of the selection process. It is not resume review or dice rolling that allows anyone to be selected in a tomorrow-focused organization.

Here, in *Leading for Tomorrow's Schools Today*, we will illustrate this method, apply our CHANGE framework, and amplify Collins' quote from the start of this chapter. Before we do that, though, we want to share the research, more than a century of industrial-organizational psychological research, upon which this is all based.

The approach to selection of staff is based upon the Big 5 Personality Theory, from John et al. (1999), explained below:

- Openness to Experience: This trait features characteristics such as imagination, insight, and a broad range of interests, reflecting a person's degree of intellectual curiosity and creativity.
- Conscientiousness: This dimension includes high levels of thoughtfulness, good impulse control, and goal-directed behaviors, indicating how organized and dependable an individual is.
- Extraversion: This trait encompasses sociability, assertiveness, and emotional expressiveness, highlighting how outgoing and energetic a person is.
- Agreeableness: This dimension involves attributes like trust, altruism, kindness, and affection, reflecting how cooperative and compassionate an individual is towards others.
- Neuroticism: This trait includes emotional instability, anxiety, moodiness, and irritability, indicating the tendency to experience negative emotions.

In the structured selection model described, an applicant takes an online assessment, or profile builder, and initial data is assembled. The applicant's responses demonstrate acknowledgment of or certain talents. This baseline data set, aligned to a construct model, in this case from Humanex Ventures research, gives the HR team an idea of talent recognition from the applicant pool. The assessments of talent are based upon and can be mapped to the Big 5 Personality Theory.

Prior to a resume review, cover letter read, essay review (all required parts of the selection process as well), the applicants are able to be categorized by talent based data. The information allows for the next stage in the selection process to make sense. Based upon the factors described, select applicants are then invited into a telephone interview that goes beyond talent identification, and into talent application. The constructs upon which the talent is derived come from data, research, evidence, and can be mapped to the Big 5 Personality traits.

Following the in-depth telephone interview, the HR team has written evidence, career/education evidence, talent recognition evidence, and talent application. Before an applicant sets foot in the organization, they have an abundance of data from which to make decisions regarding the predictive nature of their future and potential employment.

Please see Figure 2.2 for a graphic illustration of the selection process.

The applicants go into a metaphorical filter. The online screener is the computer assessment of talent. The structured interview is the telephone, in-depth interview. Following all of that data collection, the HR team conducts in-person fit interviews, based on the candidate's responses and talents as

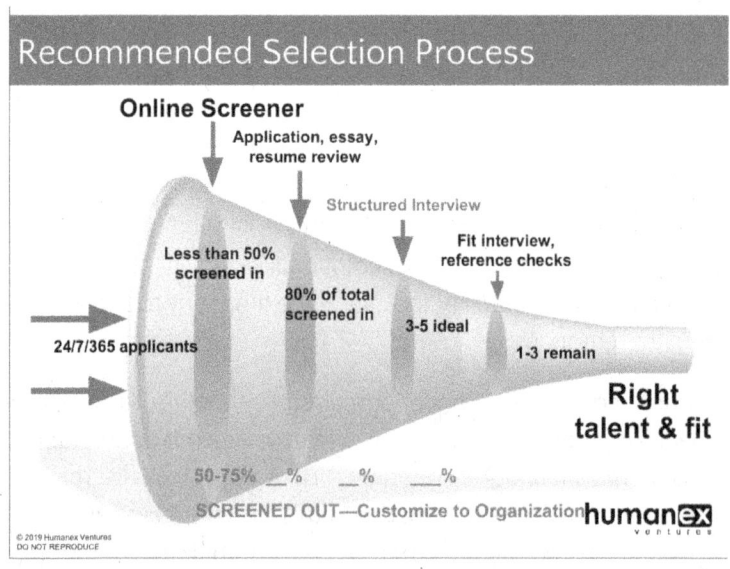

Figure 2.2 Selection process filter. *Source:* Humanex Ventures.

gathered and assessed prior to the first in-person interview. This significant investment of time and effort pays off when it comes to retention of staff (addressed later in this chapter).

Talents are found in themes of action that are related to the structured interview questions and can be mapped to the Big 5. It has been found that workstyle themes of talent measured in the models we describe are tied to or mapped to conscientiousness. Conscientiousness is more predictive of workplace performance than all other four combined.

As we started the chapter with Collins' quote, *"Great vision without great people is irrelevant."* We end the chapter with what we believe is somewhat, why, who, and how you can replicate and apply what you have learned

The impact of staff selection of staff can be measured and analyzed through organizational culture, the measure of employee satisfaction, and engagement. For an example from seven consecutive years in Mike's current school district, see Figure 2.3. Annually they measure organizational culture for all employees. The S/E shown on the y-axis in Figure 2.3 reflects the percentage of employees indicating high satisfaction and high engagement, two of the dimensions of organizational culture.

In *The Unlearning Leader*, we shared data from the United States Department of Labor regarding the improvement of predictive accuracy in organizations

Figure 2.3 Seven years of organizational culture in D112. Illustration by Michael Lubelfeld.

using structured, evidence-based selection processes. We're resharing here as an additional illustration of the statistical power of using structured selection processes to take the guesswork out of the critically important role of the HR team in getting the right people in the right seats in your organization.

By utilizing processes as described, it's possible to suggest that your reliability in making decisions goes to more than 85 percent probability! From page 62 of *The Unlearning Leader*,

> *Based on reports from Schmidt & Hunter the structured interview process helps increase this validity (of accuracy of selection of staff) by between .23 and .50. As a contrast, a selection process without scientifically based interview instruments like those found in traditional unstructured selection yields about a 30% (.30) predictive validity. Taking that .30 and adding the value of structured interviews (.51), reference checks (.26), and valuing the training and experience of candidates (.11), the whole process takes that traditional 30 and moves it up to a structured 88!*

Applying the CHANGE Leadership Framework to the evidence-based selection process case study,

- *C—Challenge the Status Quo:* The status quo for staff selection is typically reflected in a look at education/experience and resume or referral. That formula is not predictive of excellence. The challenge is to create the sense of urgency that "first who then what" is critical and that "the good old boy/girl networks" are neither good nor sustainable.
- *H—Have Open Conversations:* Discuss the commonly held beliefs about the selection of staff. Share the data, evidence, research, and results that challenge the status quo. Train and support HR teams in the selection of staff and flip the script through open, two-way dialogue.
- *A—Adapt and Be Flexible:* The adaptation is to go from the known to the unknown, the common to the uncommon. Be flexible by investing time, money, and resources in the front-end selection process. Allow the data to inform your practices. Always be people-driven and data-informed. We are not simply data-driven; we are informed by the data to allow for adaptive leadership.
- *N—Navigate Obstacles:* This takes a lot of time, energy, investment, and commitment. Navigate the obstacles of inter-rater reliability within the organization. Be sure to have courageous conversations

to make sure everyone—10 days out of 10—is doing what the organization sets forth to do.

- *G—Generate a Shared Vision:* The common vocabulary of excellence changes an organization. Hundreds of other organizations are proof of this. The shared vision is talent first and foremost, fit is second, and education/experience is tertiary, not primary. The shared vision is system-wide fidelity to the disciplined, structured process with a significant front-end investment in selection.
- *E—Enjoy the Journey:* Check the progression of organizational culture in Figure 2.3. It's very enjoyable when culture improves, when retention improves, when recruitment improves, and when selection is clear, coherent, consistent, and based on evidence.

We must note that at the time of this writing, there is a nationwide shortage of teachers and administrators. The use of structured selection methods may be an aspiration for a district where the applicant pool for specialized positions is very limited or nonexistent. With luck, grace, and good fortune, the districts referenced in the case study were slightly to moderately impacted by the shortages at the time of this writing, but we wanted to acknowledge that local conditions will impact and affect selection, recruitment, and retention.

The data in Figure 2.4 show the vacancy rates for teaching positions in Illinois in 2024.

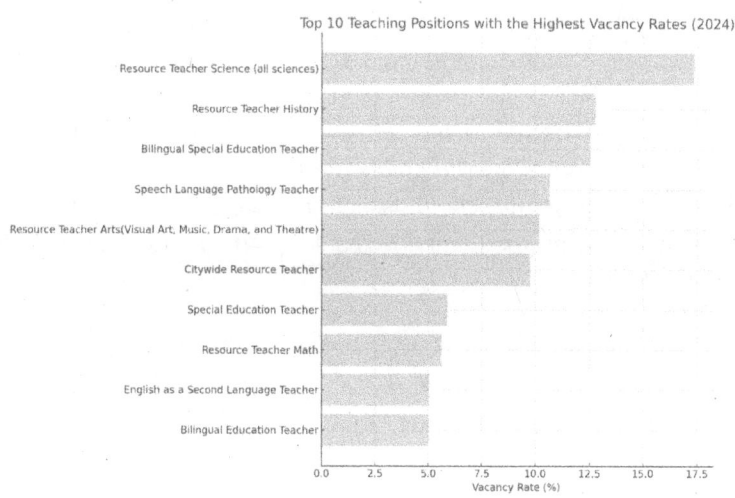

Figure 2.4 2024 Illinois vacancy rates for teaching positions. Illustration by Nick Polyak.

Selection of Staff 29

It's one thing to find teachers for your school district. It's another thing to keep them. Teacher careers can last thirty-five years or more. Ideally, people will spend those years in one district, providing continuity and leadership while maintaining a positive culture and climate into the next generation of teachers.

Back to Nick's district, there are dozens of unique school districts within miles of each other in the Chicago suburbs. The market is competitive, and the younger generation of teachers are proving to be more willing to switch districts, if not even change types of careers. When people have options, you need to start by ensuring that you have competitive wages and benefits.

Simply put, if you can help it, you never want someone to leave your district for a lateral move in order to chase more money or acquire a better benefits package.

Realistically speaking, only one district can have the highest salaries, and only one district can have the best benefits. Another way to differentiate yourself is by providing high-quality mentoring and coaching. Every new teacher needs a mentor to learn from and an instructional coach to grow professionally with. That companionship, friendship, and support can help stave off the stressors of teaching that can lead to burnout. In this same category, leaders should ensure that their evaluation model is one that supports teachers and helps them grow and develop as educators.

Leyden tries to do all of those things but decided to do something additional to improve both recruitment and retention. While doing a facility expansion and remodel, they added a preschool and day care facility inside one of their high schools. They partnered with an outside organization to rent that space and provide high-quality child care for children from six weeks to five years old. Because the school district provided the facility and pays for the associated utilities, the company is able to charge users a significantly reduced usage fee.

Now, employees of the school district know that they have a built-in, convenient option for child care. Very few school districts can boast of providing this opportunity for their staff. It's a true differentiator in a competitive job market. They suspected that this would help in recruiting and retaining staff; however, an unexpected benefit quickly surfaced. Their employees' children started to become friends, which, in turn, fostered friendships among teachers and support staff members.

The presence of the preschool and day care actually created adult relationships, play dates, and more.

That brings us to the final way to retain staff—constantly working to monitor and improve culture and morale. When people earn a livable wage with good benefits, that impacts culture. When they feel supported and have the necessary resources, that impacts culture. And when the school district uniquely meets some of their family needs, that impacts culture. When the culture is positive, people enjoy where they are and what they do, and they want to stay there. That is a great thing for students, schools, districts, and communities!

Let's look back to the reflective questions from the start of the chapter. How would you respond now, with the information we have shared?

- In what ways does your organization approach recruitment, selection, and retention of staff?
- In what ways is your organization addressing the teacher/educator shortage?
- How can you align the efforts of your community, Board of Education, Administration, faculty, and staff when it comes to hiring?
- Considering the Big 5 Personality Theory (described in this chapter), how does it impact your view of your organization's selection process?

Our youth deserve disciplined, focused, mission-driven leadership. They deserve equitable access to the best educational opportunities. Maximizing their education benefits not only the students but society as a whole.

Like the Collins quote from the beginning of the chapter, *"Great vision without great people is irrelevant,"* our case studies and leadership changes reinforce this principle that people are essential and leadership depends upon the building of and sustaining of relationships.

In this chapter, we have shared our vision and experiences, reinforcing the idea that building the right team is foundational to achieving greatness. The journey of leading for tomorrow's schools today begins with selecting the right people and creating conditions where they can thrive, ensuring our students receive the best education possible.

Voices from the Field

Leading Transformation in a VUCA World: A Progressive Vision for Brigantine Public School District

Glenn Robbins

As a progressive school superintendent at the Brigantine Public School District in Brigantine, New Jersey, my approach to leadership has been shaped by an understanding of our rapidly changing school world—a world characterized by Volatility, Uncertainty, Complexity, and Ambiguity (VUCA). Leading in this environment requires not only the capacity to manage change but also a forward-thinking mindset that embraces innovation and adapts to the evolving needs of our students and staff.

In this section, I'll delve into how our district has navigated these challenges by implementing transformative strategies that not only meet the demands of a VUCA world but also set a precedent for educational excellence. From reimagining staff schedules to pioneering ungraded classes and integrating cutting-edge technology and community partnerships, Brigantine Public School District has become a model of progressive education. These initiatives are designed to foster a culture of continuous improvement, collaborative learning, and real-world relevance.

Leadership in a VUCA World

Leading in a VUCA world requires more than traditional management skills; it demands an agile, visionary approach. This means being prepared to pivot when faced with unexpected challenges and opportunities, while also inspiring and equipping staff and students to thrive in a dynamic environment. At Brigantine, our leadership strategy involves fostering an environment where change is embraced and seen as an opportunity for growth.

One of the key aspects of our approach is ensuring that our leadership team and staff are well-prepared for the uncertainties of the future. This involves continuous professional development, strategic foresight, and a willingness to experiment with new methods and technologies. Our leadership model emphasizes transparency, open communication, and a shared vision for educational excellence, which helps to create a cohesive and resilient school community.

Implementing Innovative Scheduling for Pedagogical Development

Recognizing that effective teaching is at the heart of educational success, we have restructured our staff schedules to provide educators with dedicated time for professional growth and collaboration. This initiative, known as Extra Prep Time/Common Planning, allocates an additional period each week for teachers to focus on researching and implementing new pedagogical practices.

During this extra prep time, staff members engage in collaborative planning sessions, participate in professional development workshops, and explore the latest educational technologies and resources. This not only enhances their teaching strategies but also fosters a culture of continuous learning and innovation within the district. By prioritizing educators' professional growth, we ensure that they are equipped with the tools and knowledge needed to provide students with high-quality, relevant instruction.

Creating Ungraded Classes for Student Empowerment

In our quest to foster higher-level productivity and student engagement, we have introduced ungraded classes where scholars have the opportunity to lead and create content for the Brigantine Community School YouTube channel and several student-led podcasts on podcast platforms. These ungraded courses are designed to provide students with real-world skills and a platform to tell their own stories.

Through these initiatives, students are not only involved in content creation but also in the management and promotion of their work. They develop skills in media production, communication, and digital literacy, which are essential in today's information-driven world. Moreover, the ungraded nature of these courses allows students to explore their interests and passions without the pressure of traditional grading, fostering a more authentic and intrinsic motivation to learn.

The Brigantine Community School YouTube channel and podcasts have become valuable resources for sharing the district's achievements, student perspectives, and educational innovations. These platforms have also served as a means to engage with the broader community, showcasing the talent and creativity of our students while building a positive image of our schools.

Integrating Twenty-First-Century Skills into the Curriculum

As part of our commitment to preparing students for the future, we have incorporated cutting-edge subjects into our curriculum, such as Cybersecurity and Artificial Intelligence (AI). These courses are designed to equip middle school scholars with critical skills that are increasingly relevant in today's digital economy.

The Cybersecurity program introduces students to the fundamentals of online safety, data protection, and ethical hacking, providing them with a strong foundation in a field that is vital for both personal security and professional opportunities. Similarly, the AI curriculum explores the principles of machine learning, data analysis, and intelligent systems, preparing students for a future where AI plays a significant role in various industries.

By integrating these advanced subjects into our curriculum, we ensure that our students are not only consumers of technology but also creators and critical thinkers who can navigate and contribute to a technology-driven world.

Collaborating with the Chamber of Commerce: The Mr. Rogers Project

One of our most successful community partnerships is the Mr. Rogers Project, which involves collaboration with the local Chamber of Commerce. This initiative pairs students with local businesses to assist with social media and digital advertising, while business owners provide insights into the intricacies of running a business.

Through this project, students gain hands-on experience in digital marketing, branding, and content creation, working directly with businesses to develop and implement effective advertising strategies. This real-world application of their skills not only enhances their learning experience but also provides valuable contributions to the local economy.

Additionally, business owners benefit from fresh perspectives and innovative ideas brought by the students, creating a mutually beneficial relationship that strengthens community ties and supports local enterprises. The Mr. Rogers Project exemplifies how educational institutions and businesses can collaborate to provide meaningful learning experiences and address community needs.

Embracing Esports with the Megalodons

In response to the growing interest in esports and its potential for fostering teamwork, strategic thinking, and technological skills, the Brigantine Public School District has established its own esports team, The Megalodons. Competing in the Garden State Esports League, The Megalodons participate in three seasons throughout the year, engaging in competitive gaming that mirrors the organization and discipline found in traditional sports.

The decision to embrace esports was driven by our commitment to providing students with diverse opportunities for growth and learning. Esports, often viewed through the lens of recreational gaming, has been recognized for its ability to enhance skills such as problem-solving, collaboration, and digital literacy. The Megalodons offer students a platform to develop these skills in a structured, competitive environment.

Participation in the Garden State Esports League has provided students with valuable experiences, including strategic planning, teamwork, and resilience.

Competing against other schools not only allows students to apply their skills in a real-world context but also fosters school spirit and community engagement. The esports program has become an integral part of our district's offerings, reflecting our commitment to embracing contemporary trends and preparing students for the future.

Fostering a Positive School Culture and Climate

Creating a supportive and inclusive school environment is essential for student success and overall district effectiveness. At Brigantine, we have partnered with Humanex Ventures to measure and develop data-driven strategies for improving our school culture and climate.

Humanex Ventures provides tools and expertise for assessing various aspects of our school environment, including staff morale, student engagement, and organizational effectiveness. By analyzing this data, we are able to identify areas for improvement and implement targeted interventions that enhance our school climate.

Our focus on intentional cultural and climate development includes initiatives such as professional development for staff on cultural competency, student-led diversity and inclusion programs, and efforts to promote positive relationships and a sense of belonging among students. These efforts contribute to a nurturing and equitable learning environment where every student can thrive.

Navigating Challenges with Stoicism

Achieving success in a VUCA world is not without its challenges. The journey to transforming Brigantine Public School District has been marked by significant hurdles, including the Covid-19 pandemic, unexpected circumstances, traditional practices, and complex collective bargaining agreements. A stoic approach to leadership has been essential in overcoming these obstacles.

Stoicism, a philosophy that emphasizes resilience, control over one's reactions, and acceptance of what cannot be changed, has guided our leadership during turbulent times. For instance, the Covid-19 pandemic presented unprecedented challenges, forcing us to quickly adapt to remote learning and implement health and safety measures. Maintaining a stoic demeanor allowed us to remain focused on our goals, make pragmatic decisions, and support our staff and students through uncertainty.

Unexpected circumstances, such as sudden budget constraints or shifts in educational policy, required us to remain adaptable and proactive. By practicing stoicism, we were able to manage our responses to these challenges effectively, prioritizing solutions over problems, and maintaining a steady course toward our objectives.

Collective bargaining agreements also presented their own set of challenges. Navigating negotiations with various stakeholder groups required patience, empathy, and a commitment to finding mutually beneficial solutions. A stoic approach helped us approach these negotiations with a clear mind, focusing on long-term goals and maintaining positive relationships with our staff.

In each of these scenarios, the principles of stoicism—accepting what we cannot control, focusing on what we can influence, and maintaining inner resilience—have been instrumental in guiding our decisions and actions. This mindset has not only helped us address immediate challenges but also reinforced our commitment to our broader vision for educational excellence.

Achieving State, Regional, and National Recognition

The success of our progressive initiatives at Brigantine has not gone unnoticed. The district has garnered recognition at the state, regional, and national levels for its innovative approach to education. This recognition reflects the hard work and dedication of our entire school community, including students, staff, and partners.

Our achievements include accolades for excellence in curriculum development, scheduling changes, community engagement, and the integration of technology into teaching and learning. These honors validate the effectiveness of our strategies and serve as a testament to the positive impact of our progressive vision.

Looking ahead, we are committed to continuing our journey of transformation and improvement. Our goal is to build on our successes, expand our initiatives, and further enhance the educational experience for all students in the Brigantine Public School District.

Conclusion

Leading in a VUCA world requires adaptability, vision, and a commitment to continuous improvement. At Brigantine Public School District, we have embraced these principles through innovative scheduling, ungraded courses, advanced curriculum integration, community partnerships, esports, and a focus on school culture and climate. These efforts have not only transformed our district but also positioned us as a model for progressive education.

By sharing our experiences and strategies, we hope to inspire other school leaders to embark on their own journeys of transformation. In a world characterized by change and uncertainty, the key to success lies in our ability to innovate, collaborate, and remain steadfast in our commitment to providing the best possible education for our students.

Part II
Go Where the Smart People Are—Learning from Others

3 Networks and Professional Organizations

Before you are a leader, success is all about growing yourself. When you become a leader, success is all about growing others.

—Jack Welch

In a rapidly changing educational landscape, those who learn and adapt survive, but those who collaborate and innovate thrive. This chapter explores the critical role that networks and professional organizations play in leadership development, providing actionable strategies for leveraging these connections to drive change and foster growth. We use our own "origin story" to illustrate growth from networks and professional organizations.

Nick always says, "Let's go where the smart people are" so we can learn, grow, and expand our impact as leaders. To the smart people we have gone! Please see Figure 3.1 for an illustration of Nick and Mike's global adventures.

We have been fortunate with multiple opportunities to lead across the globe (Australia, the United Kingdom, Dominican Republic, Puerto Rico, China, and across the United States) and share our messages of unlearning, incorporating student voice, being unfinished as a leader and as a teacher, and more. Like Welch says in the quote at the start of the chapter, as leaders, our success is all about growing leaders.

Before we get too far into this chapter, we ask that you take some time to think about this chapter's reflective questions:

- Who are your go-to sources for inspiration and learning, and how have they shaped your leadership?
- Reflecting on Welch's quote, how do you balance personal growth with the responsibility of nurturing others?
- Are you actively seeking out mentors and coaches? If not, why not? In what ways can this help you grow as a leader?
- In what ways do you find growth opportunities from your professional associations?

Nick and Mike's Global Adventures

Figure 3.1 Nick and Mike's global adventures. Illustration by Michael Lubelfeld and Nick Polyak.

For a study of networks and professional organizations, and their impact, we decided to go back to the start of the Nick and Mike story! Why are we telling you our story? It is fundamental to whom we have become and we think it just might help unlock the rest of your personal leadership story.

In our second and third years as superintendents, respectively, we learned about an innovative leadership development program for early-career superintendents called ISAL, the Illinois School for Advanced Leadership. We joined a cohort in Springfield, Illinois, at the headquarters of the IASA (Illinois Association of School Administrators). Our lives and professional fortunes were forever changed by that eighteen-month leadership journey and exploration of personal and professional planning.

We were from different geographical areas, upbringings, life experiences, and professional journeys. After we met at ISAL, our journeys became inexorably linked. The ISAL cohort brought together leaders (early-career superintendents paired with master coach superintendents) and professors (from Cardinal Stritch University in Wisconsin) and addressed the geographic diversity of the state of Illinois. Deliberately and intentionally, the cohort was diverse in just about every way one can imagine.

For reference, Illinois has twelve million people in 102 counties, with five million living in Cook County (which includes Chicago). Looking at suburban

Chicago, for example, there are nine million of the twelve million people. Illinois is also geographically large, North to South—390 miles, East to West—210 miles. So, three million people inhabit a whole lot of land, and nine million people are pretty densely populated in the northeast of the state. Superintendent experiences vary widely. The networking and professional learning afforded us opportunities to work with and become friends with people we normally would not have ever seen or worked with due to vast geographical distances.

Following ISAL, we enrolled in a similar program with the American Association of School Administrators (AASA)—The National Superintendent Certification Program. For another eighteen months of leadership development, we built relationships and learned alongside superintendents from across the country. Our hearts, minds, knowledge, experiences, perspectives, abilities, and journey demonstrated and illustrated the power of networks and the depth of leadership capacity. Without those three years of personal and professional growth, none of what we have accomplished would have been the same.

Friends we have made along the way are now serving as mentors in our aspiring leadership programs. Friends from whom we learned and have grown have authored essays in the books we have written (including in this one). Leadership development and partnership have allowed us to speak across the world, serve humanity in the Dominican Republic, Puerto Rico, and Guatemala, and speak, lead, learn, and grow all over the United States. Those programs completely changed the trajectory of our careers.

We were motivated to write our first book, *The Unlearning Leader*, upon reflection from a Future Ready Conference where we heard a futurist recount examples of the need to unlearn old information to make room for new realities. He explained that it takes nearly twenty years for people to actually unlearn information that is no longer true. Twenty years is a generation of youth. A fun fact is that Tom Murray, the author of the foreword for this book, is the director for Innovation for Future Ready Schools!

As superintendents, we know that if we wait twenty years for a change to be implemented, a generation will be lost. The impact would compound. We simply cannot wait that long. Unlearning is as vital as learning in today's fast-paced world. Leaders must swiftly let go of outdated practices to make room for innovative strategies that better serve our current students.

With partnerships in state and national associations, we have been afforded the unique opportunity to both lead for and learn from networks and professional organizations. Over the years, we have co-led the IASA Aspiring Superintendent Academy in Illinois (with Dr. Courtney Orzel and Dr. Dawn Bridges), and the AASA Aspiring Superintendent Academy, Blended Learning Model. In addition, we were allowed to lead the AASA Digital Consortium which evolved into the Transformational Leadership Consortium and is now the Innovation for Transformation Consortium. We have also led the National Instructional Leadership Academy, a partnership with AVID. As we benefited from amazing networking opportunities, we are now able to lead those experiences and help connect other leaders across the state and nation.

Unfortunately, we've found that many leaders limit their connections to their school building, district, or region. Worse, many people try to go about leadership alone. Arguably, we are all busy. Arguably, we always have more work to do. Arguably, it's easier to hunker down and stay home. Our experiences show, however, one can grow into a far more impactful leader with a broader legacy when one learns beyond their own area.

Looking at "pre-networking" as the status quo, the Satir Model helps leaders navigate change to get more connected:

- *Current Status Quo*—We will start with an assumption that your current reality has you either not engaged with professional organizations and learning opportunities, or you are under-involved in the same. Prior to the ISAL and AASA experiences, our body of knowledge and field of experience were inward-looking and local. Back then, we didn't know what we didn't know. Current status quo might relate to "I'm too busy to join right now."
- *Foreign Element*—In our case, the introduction of a statewide leadership cohort, followed by the national leadership cohort, disrupted our current status quo. For you, you need to look and see what is available in your region or state. If you don't see one, start one. Take a look at the variety of leadership cohorts offered at AASA and pick one to join. The foreign element is broadening your views by jumping into a network and taking the risk to learn, lean in, and share.
- *Chaos*—Getting involved beyond your day-to-day responsibilities brings added things to do and time away from your district. With

registration costs and travel costs, you may also encounter criticism on whether or not the costs and the time are worth the benefits. As a leader, you need to make sure that your supervisor or your school board supports these efforts. You also need to consider the impact of your involvement on your family and personal sphere. Chaos is inviting new views and ideas into your setting and organization. Chaos will be change efforts you may seek to replicate and implement.

- *Integration*—As your involvement becomes the norm, you will be able to show more and more benefits to you personally and to your building or district. When you learn from other leaders, you start to use their successes and their failures to inform your work. Similarly, those other leaders are learning from your successes and failures as we all support one another. Integration will also show change in the approaches of your organization from the way it's always been done to a new view for the future. In essence, we challenge you to lead for tomorrow's schools today versus leading for yesterday's schools.

- *New Status Quo*—The new status quo is a reality where you could never imagine not being involved in professional learning across the state and nation. You can point to decisions that you've made and programs you offer your students that were copied or adapted from other districts you have encountered. The end result is improved student outcomes due to the fact that you've opened yourself up to wider learning opportunities. The new status quo is a far broader approach to leadership practices based upon new learning.

Through partnership, leadership, mentorship from so many leaders, we left our own leadership silos and took on journey after journey and adventure after adventure. From school district site visits in Washington state, Washington, DC, North Carolina, Missouri, New York, Ohio, California, Texas, Puerto Rico, the Dominican Republic, Guatemala, New Jersey, Wisconsin, Kentucky, Pennsylvania, and Illinois, we have shared and learned many transformative ideas.

We even had the opportunity to be part of an Innovation Summit at the White House in Washington, DC. By joining and getting involved in state/national level cohorts for professional learning, you can take the local chaos and get actionable ideas that you can implement in your own setting. So, what is holding you back? We never imagined that we would be engaged at the US Trademark Office—but we were, and we brought teachers with us too. We paid it forward, like Welch's quote at the start of the chapter, we supported leadership development of self and, more germane, we supported the leadership development of others.

Looking at all of this through our CHANGE Leadership Framework shares additional insights for your development and for our collective growth.

C—Challenge the Status Quo: The status quo may be you're not traveling or joining networks beyond your locale. Does the cost of travel pose a threat to the visits around the nation? That is a real and potential obstacle. We suggest seeking out professional scholarships or subsidies (business partners, professional associations), or start with a virtual model. You don't have to jump into the biggest or most expensive programs. There are also tons of video-based or web-based learning programs and cohort leadership opportunities.

Reading a book, listening to a podcast, or attending a webinar all make sense and can fill the gaps when there are financial constraints. Your community needs you to go where the smart people are, whether you can physically travel or join via modern technology. You have to reach out and learn and grow. We suggest that not doing so is not an option (sorry for the double negative, but it's for emphasis). You don't always need to travel for extended periods of time or spend large amounts of money. Those decisions we made, and the support we have had from multiple boards of education, gave us access to an abundance of innovative solutions and enhanced our own personal and professional critical thinking skills.

H—Have Open Conversations: Signing up and showing up are a great start, you also have to engage. Relationships don't make themselves, and learning doesn't happen by osmosis. In order to learn from others, and vice versa, you have to communicate with them. When you attend site visits, ask questions of the students and staff. When you attend AASA cohorts, you also have the ability to bring additional leaders from your district. This allows you to have open conversations with them, in the moment, about how your learning can benefit the students in your district.

A—Adapt and Be Flexible: When you learn from others, rarely will their solution or their program make sense to replicate in your district. You need to approach your professional connections and learning with a lens of adaptability. Ask yourself questions like, "What can I learn from what they are doing?" "How can

I adapt this idea to meet the needs of our students?" "What are my next steps to make positive change a reality?"

N—Navigate Obstacles: Obstacles for joining professional networks and professional organizations are real. They cost money to join, and some school systems cannot afford the membership fees. They cost time away from your district and your family. Some communities support and encourage this level of participation, and some do not. You need to be aware of your local context. In some communities, you can overdo it and be engaged in too many things. In other communities, you can underdo it if you don't engage in wider circles. The bottom line is that you need to navigate obstacles in the way that it makes sense for you and your district.

G—Generate a Shared Vision: While you might be the one participating in this learning, you cannot lead change alone. You need to incorporate other key leaders in your district. You need to be transparent with your school board, your colleagues, your staff, and your community. Consider sharing in a newsletter, on social media, or in a blog. This will not only help generate a shared vision but also allow others to see the benefit of getting involved to bring good ideas back to the district.

E—Enjoy the Journey: While change can be challenging, it's important to remember to celebrate the small wins and enjoy the process. Our many trips and adventures are not just about learning new strategies but also about building relationships, fostering a sense of camaraderie, and reigniting a passion for teaching and learning. The time spent together, both in professional settings and during informal moments, helps to strengthen bonds and create a positive atmosphere that will carry forward into the implementation phase. We have seen firsthand that laughing together supports learning together!

As we close out this chapter about networks and professional organizations, we go back to the reflection questions from the beginning of the chapter.

- Who are your go-to sources for inspiration and learning, and how have they shaped your leadership?
- Reflecting on Welch's quote, how do you balance personal growth with the responsibility of nurturing others?

- Are you actively seeking out mentors and coaches? If not, why not? In what ways can this help you grow as a leader?
- In what ways do you find growth opportunities from your professional associations?

The impact of networking has allowed us to lead globally, mentor others, and continuously grow alongside like-minded leaders. Programs like ISAL provided us with not just professional development but a partnership that has driven our leadership journey. By learning from different regions, cultures, and experiences, we realized how much we didn't know and how essential it is to seek out those who challenge and inspire us.

As educational leaders, the future of our schools depends on our ability to learn, unlearn, and lead boldly. Let's commit to taking the steps necessary today to ensure a thriving tomorrow for our students. We must impact our schools today so that we can have the best tomorrow possible. We do not need to wait—we cannot wait!

4 Language Matters

If you talk to a man in a language he understands, that goes to his head. If you talk to him in his language, that goes to his heart.

—Nelson Mandela

No matter where you go in the United States, schools share certain staples—classrooms, cafeterias, libraries. Students study the core subjects of reading, writing, math, and science. But what unites nearly all schools across the country is the language used in those classrooms: English.

Many schools across the United States serve students and families who speak a variety of languages, and in some cases, English isn't the dominant language. What if we allowed students to perform on stage in the language most meaningful or most comfortable to them? That is exactly what happened at Leyden Community High School District 212 when they created Teatro Leyden.

Before we go into that story, the case study for this chapter, let's start with the following reflective questions:

- How do you meet the diverse language needs of your students and families?
- How can your district celebrate linguistic diversity rather than merely addressing it?
- How does language present a barrier to some of your students from being fully engaged in the school experience?
- Does your school district program to address language differences or celebrate language differences?
- In what areas can your district remove barriers related to home languages so that everyone feels welcome and included in the school district?

As we shared earlier, Nick's district at Leyden serves approximately 3,500 high school students in suburban Chicago. Of those students, over 70 percent identify as Hispanic. In 2013, the theater department made an interesting observation. The vast majority of students in the district were Hispanic; however, that student population was significantly underrepresented on stage in the district's theater productions. That prompted them to ask a transformative question, "What if we offered theater in both English and Spanish?"

They had come across a production called *La Gringa* that provided scripts in both languages. *La Gringa* is the story of a young girl named Maria who was born in Puerto Rico. As a child, she moved to New York, but she never felt like she fit in as a Puerto Rican in the United States. As a teenager, she decided to go back to Puerto Rico to learn about her family's roots. While there, she didn't feel like she fit in because she was seen as a mainland American in Puerto Rico. Effectively, she was a young woman caught between two cultures, caught between two worlds; she no longer fit in with either.

This story resonated with many of Leyden's students and Teatro Leyden was born. Students tried out for the play regardless of whether their first language was Spanish or English. Two casts were chosen and some bilingual students even set out to perform in both shows. The combined cast rehearsed together and when it came time for the curtain to rise, attendees could choose whether they wanted to see the production in English or Spanish.

The language barrier for getting involved in their high school activities was now gone. One student participant said, "I think if there was no Spanish cast, I would not have had the courage to try out in another language." Clearly, this benefited students and opened doors for participation. The district hadn't really thought about an additional benefit: community involvement.

Figure 4.1 Poster for the play *La Gringa*, a production that can be performed in both Spanish and English. *Source:* Nick Polyak.

All of a sudden, Teatro Leyden posters were showing up in different restaurants and stores throughout the community where more of the Spanish-speaking population frequented. And on the opening nights, they saw new and different community members walking through the door who could see the students perform in their native language. In reflecting on that first year, one of the actor's parents said, "It is very good to have the theater in both English and Spanish, because this way, the Hispanic community gets more involved in the social activities and school activities."

Now, Teatro Leyden had an identity and a head of steam. In the years that followed, they found show after show where they could double-cast the productions and allow students to shine on stage regardless of whether their first language was English or Spanish. In 2018, the program caught the eye of the National Association of School Boards. They designated Teatro Leyden as their Grand Prize Magna Award winner for the top equity program in the country. The students rose to celebrity status with videos made and articles written about them. And as part of the award, the group was given a prize of $10,000.

Nick went to the theater department and asked them how they wanted to spend that money. Fully expecting them to want to refinish the floor, buy costumes, or get new lights, he was surprised by their response. Instead of asking to buy things, they asked if they could commission a Latina playwright in Chicago to create a brand new show just for their kids. This request led to a partnership with playwright Nancy Garcia Loza.

The end product was a brand new show called *Wave*. It's a story about the emotional toll it takes on families transitioning from other countries to the United States. In truth, it's the story of many of the kids at Leyden and all across the country. Nancy didn't just write the show; she partnered with the student thespians at Leyden to support the creative process. They helped workshop ideas and participated in re-writes. When the show was finally completed, the students in Teatro Leyden were able to perform the world premiere of the show they helped create.

When Teatro Leyden celebrated its tenth anniversary in 2023, they once again performed *La Gringa* to pay homage back to the start of this program that changed the way kids can engage in their high school. It was also a celebration of all of the schools that have heard their story and created similar opportunities for the students in their schools. This case study links directly to Mandela's quote from the start of the chapter, "If you talk to a man in a language he understands, that goes to his head. If you talk to him in his language, that goes to his heart."

Before we personalize this story down to an individual student, let's take a look at how this works in the Satir Model of Change:

- *Status Quo:* Prior to 2013, Leyden's theater program looked and operated like just about every program in schools around the country. If you didn't speak English, or if you weren't yet confident in your English-speaking skills, the doors to the theater were closed to you. And the significant number of parents and community members who primarily spoke English would not or could not attend the shows at the schools because they wouldn't be able to understand.

- *Foreign Element:* In this case, a school counselor and play director named Bill Mitchell looked at the current reality and asked the question—What if? The theater director found a show that would make this possible, and the administration gave permission to try something different.

- *Chaos:* The idea is great in concept, and then the realities start to set in. There are a lot more kids to manage. There were some kids rehearsing in one language, others rehearsing in another, and yet other students trying to take part in both casts. Very few of the adults involved spoke Spanish, and they were trying to give stage directions and help students with timing and blocking. The execution of the program involved significantly more than the original idea.

- *Integration:* The theater department made two big decisions to get help with integration. They brought on a Spanish teacher from the language department to help work with students on their lines and their delivery. More importantly, they empowered student directors to help become leaders for their fellow castmates. When all of the pieces came together, Teatro Leyden became not only manageable but very successful.

- *New Status Quo:* Over a decade later, Teatro Leyden is a fixture in the school community. They have performed at the State Theater Festival and conducted workshops to help other districts adopt a similar model. They are a testament to the power of a single question and the importance of being reflective of the needs and wants of your local community.

On the programmatic level, it would seem hard to argue about the importance of programs like this. However, as we teased earlier, the story gets even stronger when you look at it through the lens of an individual student.

In 2013, there was a freshman at Leyden (we'll call her Ana) who was new to both the school district and the country. Ana grew up in Guatemala with her parents, her two sisters, and her brother. In the years leading up to this, their family experienced great change and great trauma. Her oldest sister came to the United States to study and ended up meeting someone, getting married, and staying in the United States. Her brother was involved in an argument that turned violent and he was tragically shot and killed. Finally, her other sister went out one day with her boyfriend, and they both disappeared.

Ana's parents were torn with grief. They didn't want her to stay in Guatemala due to the dangers that befell her siblings, but they also knew they couldn't leave their home in hopes that her sister would return. With all of that, they made the difficult decision to send Ana to live with her sister in the United States while they stayed behind. Ana left behind her school, friends, and family, unsure if she'd ever feel at home in this new world where she didn't speak the language. This is the story of how Ana arrived at Leyden.

Her Spanish teacher gave her the script and told her she would be trying out for a play that week. Likely not fully understanding all of what was happening, Ana did as she was asked. She tried out for *La Gringa* and she was given the leading role in the Spanish language version. Ana, who was transitioning from her life in Guatemala to a life in the United States would be playing Maria who was caught between her lives in New York and Puerto Rico. This story of a young woman caught between two worlds echoed the realities that many Leyden students faced, straddling their Hispanic roots and their American surroundings

As I'm sure you guessed, she and the whole cast were amazing. Ana went on to star in Teatro Leyden productions all four years. She and her friends even founded a student group called the ExcELLence Club. If you note that capital ELL, their focus was on helping other students who are learning English find ways to get involved in their high schools. As a bit of a post-script, Ana is currently studying to be a high school teacher and she's been told that there is always a job waiting for her back at Leyden.

Let's look at how Ana's story can analyzed through utilization of the CHANGE Leadership Framework:

- *C—Challenge the Status Quo:* Ana, labeled as an ELL student, wouldn't have traditionally considered theater an option. It took one visionary adult to challenge that assumption, opening up unimaginable possibilities.

- *H—Have Open Conversations:* Your school district needs to allow, encourage, and celebrate the free exchange of ideas. In the conversations that led to Teatro Leyden, there was no talk of what extra costs might occur. No one asked if the community might push back against Spanish language theater. The open conversation in this case was simply one revolving around what's best for the kids.

- *A—Adapt and Be Flexible:* Change requires flexibility. When you create two casts for a show, that means that all of the kids will only get half of the eventual stage time for performances. Empowering student directors and language teachers helped get over some of the hurdles in this case.

- *N—Navigate Obstacles:* One of the biggest obstacles for Teatro Leyden has been the fact that not many scripts exist in both English and Spanish. It's not as simple as running an English script through a language translator because many of the jokes and nuances can easily get lost. That was a large driver for the group to create *Wave* with Nancy Garcia Loza. If the scripts don't exist, then we'll just have to create them ourselves.

- *G—Generate a Shared Vision:* Leyden's mission statement is Educate, Enrich, Empower: Student and Communities. In that word "enrich" is the idea that there is something for everyone at their high schools. Without allowing Spanish-speaking students an opportunity to perform in their language, we were fundamentally violating that shared vision.

- *E—Enjoy the Journey:* There is nothing better, in terms of enjoying the journey, than sitting in the audience and watching the joy on the students' faces and the pride from their families. Talking to Ana about her experiences and how it impacted her desire to pursue teaching is literally what our profession is all about.

With this story in mind, let's revisit the reflective questions of this chapter:

- How do you meet the diverse language needs of your students and families?
- How does language present a barrier to some of your students from being fully engaged in the school experience?
- How can your district celebrate linguistic diversity rather than merely addressing it?
- Does your school district program to address language differences or celebrate language differences?
- In what areas can your district remove barriers related to home languages so that everyone feels welcome and included in the school district?

As we have shared the story of Teatro Leyden around the state and country, one common response resonates and it's always something like this, "That's such a simple idea, why aren't we doing that?!" Leading for tomorrow's schools today requires us to look to our students and community with a sense of empathy and understanding. What do they need from us? Who do we need to be for them? What resources do we need to provide? What opportunities do we need to create?

The exact answers to those questions are different in every school district across the country. But there are commonalities where we can all learn from one another. Spanish language theater may not be a relevant need in your community, but we guarantee you that something else is. Are you creating an environment where people ask those critical questions and know they will be supported and celebrated? Your Ana is already walking through your school doors, full of untapped potential. Will you create the opportunities to unlock it? Your leadership can make all the difference.

Voices from the Field

My Journey of People-Centered Leadership as Superintendent

Zandra Jo Galván

Throughout my eight years as superintendent at Greenfield USD and now as the superintendent of the Salinas Union High School District in Monterey County, California, I have been guided by a simple but powerful philosophy: people and relationships are at the heart of every successful initiative. Building a strong network of partnerships—both within our community and across the nation—is essential to creating sustainable, positive change for students and team members in every organization. From connecting with other visionary leaders through AASA, ALAS, CALSA, ACSA, Digital Promise, and Future Ready Schools to collaborating closely with families and labor partner groups, I have witnessed how these connections have fostered supportive environments centered on student and staff well-being and success.

Creating a Community of Vision and Support

When I began my journey at Greenfield in 2017, I recognized that meaningful transformation would require a culture of openness and trust. One of the first ways I nurtured this culture was through developing a cohesive and coherent strategic plan with our governance team and staff. This plan launched our #AllmeansAll, #GreenfieldGuarantee, #GUSDproud, and #BetterTogether initiatives. Furthermore, our vision was sustained and focused through opportunities to celebrate our success by aligning practices with vision. A few ways to share our progress were "60 Seconds in GUSD," "Weekly messages from the superintendent," and "Empowered Learners with Supt Bedtime Storytime" where staff and students read to their younger siblings. These were weekly initiatives where staff and I shared updates with families and the community. In each video, I celebrated student and teacher successes, addressed challenges, and provided our community with a sense of the district's vision and mission. These updates allowed us to rally around shared commitments to our students and community.

The impact of "60 Seconds in GUSD" was felt immediately. I remember featuring a student who had struggled to adjust to remote learning. His story highlighted our efforts to provide safe study spaces, and it resonated with parents, who began reaching out for support. This student-focused approach and others built trust within our community, helping families and staff see themselves as essential contributors to each child's success.

People First: Building a Strong Partnership with Labor

When the pandemic hit, my weekly meetings with labor partner groups, staff, and community members became a cornerstone of our approach. Rather than routine check-ins, these meetings provided teachers, classified teams, administrators, and parents a space to share their concerns and offer insights on how best to support students. In response to their feedback, we implemented flexible scheduling and wellness resources that helped address the stress of teaching during such turbulent times.

This collaboration wasn't just about logistics; it created an environment of psychological safety where staff felt heard and valued. By leveraging emotional intelligence and empathy, we supported one another and remained focused on our students' needs.

One story that stands out is when teachers expressed a need for more mental health resources to help manage the pressures of hybrid instruction. We worked together to create wellness check-ins and access to counseling and social services. These partnerships were instrumental in building the resilience our staff needed to keep our students engaged and connected.

Families as Essential Partners in Student Success

One of the most important relationships we built was with our students' families. I saw parents not just as stakeholders but as essential partners in their children's learning. We implemented family town halls and virtual workshops, making it easier for families to stay involved. These events addressed parents' challenges head-on, empowering them to support their children's education, even as the learning environment shifted.

A powerful example came from a mother who attended every workshop we offered. She was eager to support her three children's online learning but initially struggled with technology. With the support of our bilingual workshops, she not only learned to navigate online platforms but also inspired other families to engage as well. Her children thrived because their family was so actively involved, and she became a community ambassador, encouraging others to participate in district events. Stories like these reinforced my commitment to family partnerships and demonstrated their profound impact on student success.

Learning from National Networks: AASA, ALAS, CALSA, ACSA, Digital Promise, and Future Ready

Throughout my career, I have found tremendous value in connecting with other leaders who share my commitment to student-centered education. Organizations like AASA (The School Superintendents Association) and ALAS (Association of Latino Administrators and Superintendents) became invaluable communities. Through AASA, I leaned into the strength of my brother and sister superintendents and learned strategies that guided our district through the abrupt shift to remote learning, while ALAS connected me with leaders who were equally focused on Latino equity and culturally responsive education. These insights were crucial as we worked to serve Greenfield's diverse student population.

When it came to implementing digital solutions, my involvement with Future Ready and Digital Promise's League of Innovative Schools made all the difference. Future Ready Schools provided frameworks to help us ensure that every student had access to online learning. Through the League of Innovative Schools, I found tools to assess digital equity in our community. Armed with this knowledge, we launched initiatives like mobile hotspots and community Wi-Fi hubs, ensuring that students without reliable internet access could still fully participate in their learning.

These solutions weren't just about overcoming logistical challenges; they reflected our belief that every student deserves equitable access to education. Future Ready Schools also helped us introduce digital citizenship workshops, equipping our students with the skills to navigate online spaces responsibly. This national connection allowed me to bring real, immediate benefits to my district.

Empowering Students with a Graduate Profile Framework

A key focus of our work in Greenfield was creating an environment that emphasized student empowerment and future readiness. We developed a "Graduate Profile" framework that identified essential skills each student should possess upon graduation, from critical thinking and adaptability to strong communication skills. By aligning our practices and purpose with our Graduate Profile, we ensured that each student's learning experience contributed to a future-focused skill set with durable, essential skills. This profile became a central part of our vision for student empowerment, providing a clear roadmap for students, parents, and staff alike.

One of the most impactful examples of this focus was the launch of my superintendent student advisory and mentorship program, where local professionals guided students on career and life skills outlined in the Graduate Profile. I'll always remember a student whose family had never had college experience. She thrived under this program, gained essential skills, and ultimately developed extreme confidence and a desire to attend a four-year university. This achievement highlighted the profound impact of a clear, skill-centered vision on students' lives.

Looking Ahead: My 100-Day Plan for Salinas UHSD

As I step into my new role as superintendent of Salinas UHSD in 2024, I carry forward the vision and values shaped by my time successfully leading in Greenfield. My experience has shown me that lasting change begins with strong relationships and a commitment to centering students in everything we do.

To establish a strong foundation in Salinas, I have crafted a 100-day plan that focuses on building relationships, assessing current needs, and setting strategic goals. During this period, I have engaged with staff, students, families, and community partners to gather input and insights that will inform our priorities moving forward.

The focus will be on three core areas:

1. Establishing Trust and Communication: I will host community forums and listening sessions to foster open dialogue and build trust. This step is crucial for creating an inclusive environment where all voices are heard and valued.

2. Assessing Needs and Resources: I will conduct a thorough evaluation of existing programs, services, and resources to identify areas of strength and opportunities for growth. This assessment will guide our strategic planning efforts.

3. Setting a Vision for Empowerment: Building on my experience with the Graduate Profile, I aim to develop a clear vision for student empowerment and future readiness in Salinas. This vision will involve collaboration with partners to ensure alignment with community needs and aspirations.

With my experience in Greenfield and the insights I've gained from my national networks, I am confident that this plan will set Salinas UHSD on a path toward innovative, student-centered practices that empower our learners for the future.

A Legacy of Relationship-Driven Success

Reflecting on my journey in Greenfield, I am proud of the culture we built together. Every achievement was rooted in the strength of our partnerships—with staff, families, labor partner groups, and colleagues from across the country. I have learned that when people feel connected to a shared purpose, they are empowered to contribute more fully to each student's success.

Using the CHANGE Framework to Reflect on My Leadership Journey:

- *Challenge the Status Quo:* My work with the Graduate Profile framework sought to redefine success metrics in Greenfield USD and Salinas UHSD, aiming beyond traditional academic outcomes.
- *Have Open Conversations:* Weekly and monthly labor partner meetings foster psychological safety and transparency, allowing teachers and classified teams to express concerns and contribute solutions.
- *Adapt and Be Flexible:* Our rapid response strategies during the pandemic and in times of crisis—like adapting learning structures for accessibility—demonstrated our commitment to flexibility.
- *Navigate Obstacles:* Overcoming barriers to digital equity required leveraging resources from networks like Future Ready Schools and Digital Promise, which provided essential frameworks.
- *Generate a Shared Vision:* The Strategic Plan and Graduate Profile served as shared roadmaps, keeping all educational partners aligned and focused on student empowerment.
- *Enjoy the Journey:* I cherish the community-building efforts that created lasting bonds and a resilient culture, elements I now bring to Salinas UHSD.

Together, we can create educational environments where every child feels valued, supported, and empowered to thrive. My leadership is grounded in a commitment to excellence, driven by the belief that relationships and partnerships are the foundation of our success. With passion, empathy, and a dedication to unity, I strive to build connections that elevate our schools and strengthen our community. This journey is one I am deeply honored to continue, knowing that every partnership, rooted in kindness and shared vision, brings us closer to a brighter future for every student I serve.

Part III
You Can Do It

5 We're Not Broke, We're Broken

Leadership and learning are indispensable to each other.
—John F. Kennedy

Throughout this chapter, Kennedy's quote will come to life. Through trial and error and through learning, District 112 went from failure to success in a relatively short period of time. In 2016, a failed referendum and an unsuccessful district leadership and governance model led to widespread community discontent. It drove out the superintendent, board members, and central office administrators, and it caused the Chicago Tribune to write that this failure was causing a civil war in Highland Park.

Mike introduced the phrase, "we're not broke, we're broken," and upon taking over as superintendent on July 1, 2018, he pledged to rebuild trust and restore the district's reputation and effectiveness. Reflecting on the District's past few years of turmoil and tragedy, he addressed the community in a town hall meeting in February 2018, where he first used this phrase. Together, the community pulled together and restored its pride, success, and future-focused leadership and governance approaches.

In 2017 when Mike was hired, Mike promised to "restore excellence" to the District, the Town Hall meeting in February put life into that quote.

In the case study shared in this chapter, we show how an organization went from rock bottom back up to success and pride in a short timeframe. These challenges beg several important questions for any leader to consider. Please consider these reflective questions:

- In what ways has community input shifted priorities and impacted your leadership?
- How do you look at historic decisions in your organization to help guide your future planning?
- How has strategic planning unified your community toward a shared purpose?
- What priorities and urgent needs exist in your organization right now?

As background, Mike's district was born out of a crisis in the 1990s. Three previously independent and separate school districts in two cities covering a land mass of less than 15 square miles, serving around 35,000 people, consolidated into one entity. The consolidation was unwelcome in the community and became a challenging, even negative experience. From *Chicago Tribune* news archives,

> *The consolidation, only the fourth in the northern suburbs since the late 1970s, was approved by 54 percent of the voters in Tuesday`s binding referendum. School Districts 107, 108 and 111 will merge on July 1, 1993.*

Beyond the politics of it all, the long-deferred maintenance of more than twelve aging school buildings had taken a toll financially and would foreshadow significant turmoil for the newly combined district. Compounded, but not as public, twelve independent schools with decentralized curricula became a less known, but as important, series of cracks in the foundation of the school system fledgling to become strong.

In 1997, a bond issue raised $40,000,000 and the district rebuilt one of the oldest and most dilapidated schools for $15,000,000, and then distributed the remaining twenty-five million dollars "equally" and not equitably. That decision, well-intentioned and quite frankly required based on the political realities of the time, would bring the organization to its knees many years later. The district also invested $10,000,000 in fund reserves toward that long-deferred maintenance. From 1997 through 2016, there would be no clear path forward out of the deferred maintenance quagmire.

In 2016 a referendum failed and it took until 2022, with a three-phase Long Range Facilities Plan, for success to once again come to Highland Park's elementary schools.

From the district's inception in 1992 through 2014, the district had five superintendents. From 2016, through Mike's selection in 2017 for the 2018 school year, there had been four acting superintendents after a superintendent departed mid-year in December. The district was in crisis when Mike arrived.

These years and events are shown in Figure 5.1

In 2018, the district was chaotic and resistant to change. They did not like the failed plan from 2016, they did not care for the people in charge, and they were emotionally exhausted. In the Status Quo, in 2016–17, prior to the new superintendent taking office, the Board of Education and the Interim

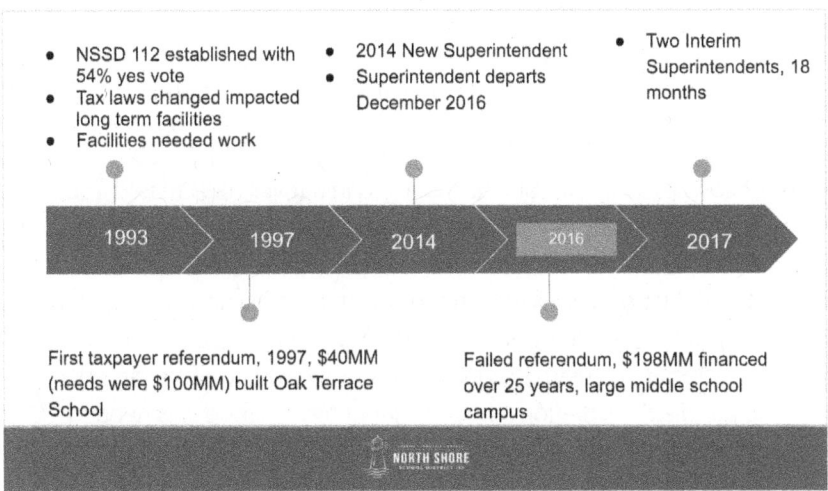

Figure 5.1 Timeline from 1993 to 2017. Illustration by Michael Lubelfeld.

Superintendents closed two of the District's twelve operating schools and made boundary changes that affected and impacted six of the neighborhood school communities.

They showed brave leadership, and this was step one in their listening to the community. The community said no to the bloated, unaligned plans from 2016, and said, "We've had enough." There was a ton of chaos when the foreign element was introduced. In this case, the foreign element was the team of the Board of Education and a newly hired superintendent. These effective interim superintendents also helped the newly configured Board of Education to see that curriculum decentralization had caused educational dysfunction as well as facilities dysfunction. Much-needed change was on the horizon.

Let's see how the Satir Model of Change applies to this case study in leadership:

- *Current Status Quo:* The district was stuck in ineffective practices with the December 2016 departure of the superintendent, leaving the district with two interim superintendents, a board of education in disarray, and a central administration in chaos. The facilities were still old, aging, in disrepair, and in need of a plan.
- *Foreign Element:* In this case, there was a high degree of administrative leadership change, including the hiring of a new superintendent. Mike was a foreign element, but he was also known due to the fact he had

worked in the district previously in his career. There was also considerable change on the School Board. So the foreign element in this story is the whole leadership team, the newly reconstituted Board, and the dual focus areas of facilities and finance and curriculum and instruction.

- *Chaos:* Leadership changes and failed initiatives had created a sense of turmoil and stagnation. Hope was elusive, trust with labor unions had eroded, and building administrators lacked clear direction. Relations with the labor unions were fraught with mistrust and adversity, and the building administrators did not know what the direction was. This new leadership team was learning how to work together and how to handle the situations they had inherited. Change was needed, but there was no trust or confidence in leadership. So there was a lot to overcome. Prior to the foreign element of the new superintendent, a major overhaul of the English language arts and Dual Language, Two-Way Immersion programming (Spanish/English) was also taking place, not to mention the closing of two beloved and historic schools, one from 1869 and the other from 1909). Chaos—indeed!

- *Integration:* Mike's arrival and partnership with the Board of Education and the community marked a shift toward rebuilding trust and governance. The interim superintendents helped reframe the board's vision. The existing administrators banded together with the hope that a new leadership approach would move the district forward, and it did! Mike and the Board created a Long-Range Planning Committee. This was composed of individuals who supported the referendum in 2016, people who opposed that same referendum, and folks in between. In addition, Mike's first year marked a year where two closed schools and all the students, parents, staff, and administrators were integrated across the district. Integration of people, ideas, new curriculum, and the new superintendent literally calling to action a Long Range Planning Committee on July 2nd started a process of integration all over the place.

- *New Status Quo:* Through intense community engagement and shared vision, the district achieved stability and progress in a remarkably short period of time. With alacrity, outreach, fervor, aggressive leadership, and expert partners, the district broke free of the malaise of failure into a new reality of success. From July 2018 through October 2018, a plan emerged that would show proof of concept. The Long-Range Facilities Plan, Phase 1, called for the upgrade and modernization of both of the middle schools, with no dedicated tax increase. It would show the community that its elected and appointed officials were listening and leading in concert with their shared values. Writing this book in the seventh year of Mike's administration also yields the highest levels of achievement across the board on the state of IL annual assessments.

Mike took the helm of his broken but not financially "broke" organization and began with a huge focus on building trust again and moving the district forward. He was interested in moving fast toward the creation of a transforming idea. The status quo of despair and general chaos was in effect upon his arrival. His approaches were ambitious and aggressive and the Board was in full support—cautiously optimistic and carefully overseeing the new status quo.

Broken was trust. Broken was clarity of focus and purpose. Broken was the Board/Superintendent/Community partnership. The idea was that they could be successful. The idea was that they are leaders. And the idea was that they could and would repair everything that was broken. Their approach restored hope, faith, and confidence in the community—quickly (before Covid and before a mass shooting in their community). They did not do this alone, no leaders ever do. They asked for help, a lot of it! And they listened! And they acted in concert with the community.

As Kennedy's quote at the start of this chapter suggests, leaders are learners. There will be ideation, success, and failure in the process. Kennedy implores those in leadership positions to be learners and to keep their curiosity alive as they delve into change management. Leading for tomorrow's schools calls for leadership itself to be inherent. The age-old challenge is creating conditions in the present that allow for the future to be realized and impacted.

Analyzing this change process using the Satir Change Model, the district navigated these challenges by focusing on governance, fiscal responsibility, and authentic community engagement. A third-party survey provided valuable insights, leading to a new status quo characterized by equity, high-quality instruction, dedicated staff, modern facilities, and a consistent curriculum. This transformation demonstrates the power of shared leadership and community collaboration.

In 2016, the District had unsuccessfully presented a comprehensive District reorganization plan and a $200,000,000 referendum ballot initiative based upon extensive planning and community engagement from 2011 to 2016.

When community engagement is ignored, that is not effective community engagement. There is no intent to disparage anyone with that statement. The reality is that the board, administration and community were engaged, but at opposite ends of desire. The Board, administration, and community were not aligned. The Board went forward anyway. The Board lost, as did a generation of students, parents, and the entire community. Their aims were the same as the aims of all Boards—high-quality, equitable educational access for all learners. Their approach, though, was not aligned with the desires of the community. They were not wrong, per se, but the approach was.

One major leadership takeaway is that it's not enough to simply have "community engagement." The leadership team must integrate, engage, listen, and ideate with that input. Successful community engagement led to a complete turnaround in this organization. The failure of the 2011–16 process was not due to lack of effort, vision, intensity, and hard work. The failure was lack of alignment with community values, wishes, desires, beliefs, and willingness to embrace certain versions of change. Communication is a two-way endeavor.

The post-failure of 2016 interim superintendents were highly effective, award-winning veterans. They helped the newly formed board understand that facilities were not the only problem. The real problem was that there was no teaching and learning infrastructure. Yes, there were aging, dilapidated buildings in dire need of upgrade too, but the main focus needed to be equitable access to educational opportunities for all children. The financial hemorrhage felt by decades of deferred maintenance made it appear that the facilities and finance issues were the problem. That distraction and interruption of the focus was the problem.

In order to get back to where they needed to be, the germane focus of student learning, facilities and finance issues needed to be addressed. This had to be done with community involvement and support, and with administrative listening and integrating the ideas from all partners. In 2017, they adopted unified curriculum resources (seemingly unimportant or mundane in many settings, but here—it was truly historic). The formerly three distinctive, unique, independent, and reluctant partners, facing tremendous challenges financially and with facilities, finally, for the first time, had a roadmap toward a guaranteed and viable curriculum.

From July 2018 through November 2018 the District worked with a third-party survey provider and the community to exchange thoughts about the

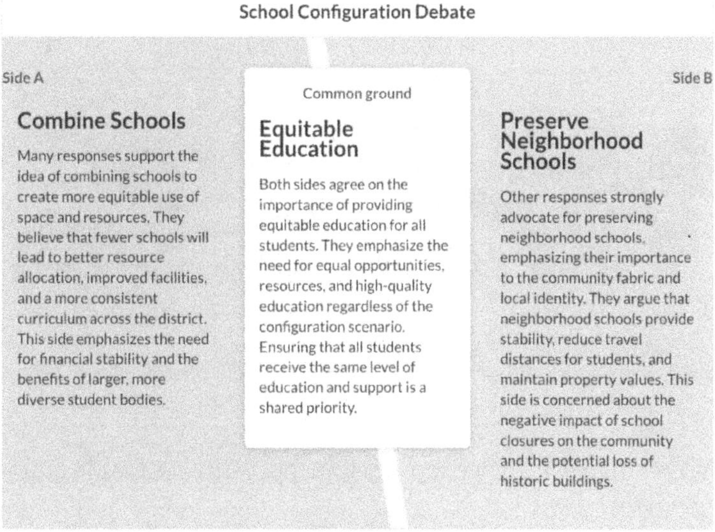

School Configuration Debate

Side A

Combine Schools

Many responses support the idea of combining schools to create more equitable use of space and resources. They believe that fewer schools will lead to better resource allocation, improved facilities, and a more consistent curriculum across the district. This side emphasizes the need for financial stability and the benefits of larger, more diverse student bodies.

Common ground

Equitable Education

Both sides agree on the importance of providing equitable education for all students. They emphasize the need for equal opportunities, resources, and high-quality education regardless of the configuration scenario. Ensuring that all students receive the same level of education and support is a shared priority.

Side B

Preserve Neighborhood Schools

Other responses strongly advocate for preserving neighborhood schools, emphasizing their importance to the community fabric and local identity. They argue that neighborhood schools provide stability, reduce travel distances for students, and maintain property values. This side is concerned about the negative impact of school closures on the community and the potential loss of historic buildings.

Figure 5.2 Debate over consolidation. Illustration by Michael Lubelfeld.

"configuration" subject. They used the results with the Long-Range Planning Committee as they built a configuration plan approved by the Board of Education in November 2018.

For a time, there was still a blur in the community as to what the district vision really was. This was a time of change. In the survey, the community also reinforced their beliefs in equity. Beliefs that would serve them well as they made very impactful decisions on facilities, finance, and the overall well-being of students and staff for years to come. In Figure 5.3, you'll see how common ground can be reached from divergent opinions. The extreme group views were those in favor of school consolidation and those with concerns. The common ground was a need for equitable education.

The transformative power of finding common ground and shared purposes allowed the district and its community to heal and realign. The district is leading for tomorrow's schools today by aligning its focus to what is really in the best interests of the students and the community.

As it shows in Figure 5.2, the community was clear; all members of the fractured community wanted all students to have access to a high-quality education. With that charge in hand, the superintendent, the Board and administration,

Moving from old to new building!

Figure 5.3 Before and after image of Northwood Middle School, 1960s–2021. *Source:* Michael Lubelfeld.

and the community marched forward together with a renewed purpose and sense of hope.

The survey prompt asked the community: "What are the most important perspectives that we must take into account while planning for potential changes in our facilities and school boundaries?" After analyzing the results of the 930 people, 1,081 thoughts, and 52,526 ratings, the following themes and concepts emerged as common ground uniting the community's input:

- Equity: Inclusiveness. Every child in District 112 deserves to have the same educational opportunities, no matter what schools they attend in the district.
- Instruction and Curriculum: Our students need high-quality instruction so they can be well-informed critical thinkers and conscientious citizens.
- Teachers and Staff: Creating an environment where excellent administrators, teachers, and staff want to come and spend their careers here. Continuity is important for our students, our curriculum, and our community.
- Twenty-first-century Facilities: Updated facilities. Students deserve a twenty-first-century learning environment.
- Consistent Curriculum: Develop a standard curriculum while also providing learning opportunities for students who are at either high or low ends of the range to engage and challenge. We want to develop all students to their full potential, and not prioritize standardized test results over fully developed critical and creative thinkers.

These five clarion calls were generated from common ground—people with polar opposite views (those who supported the failed referendum in 2016 and those who opposed it) all agreed to these five concepts. This is integration, vis-à-vis Satir, at its finest. This is G, Generate a Shared Vision, in the CHANGE Leadership Framework.

The new approach in 2018 was akin to a quote from Theodore Roosevelt: "Do what you can, with what you have, where you are." This quote captured the spirit of the opportunities they had in the district at this time. The problems in front of the district were simply too large to be fixed with one plan. Neither the problems nor the solutions were easy.

The old status quo had been failing. The new status quo became a success. District leadership and the community knew that they had the responsibility and great opportunity to do what they needed to do. They would make changes to improve educational outcomes, facilities, and equity, one step at a time.

Nonetheless, they were thrilled to be able to proffer a plan that took existing resources with no dedicated tax increase and made dramatic improvements to the school district. District planning took an estimated $75,000,000 project renovating both middle schools with $20,000,000 in fund balance reserves and $55,000,000 in alternate revenue bonds.

The bonds would be paid back by the operations funds, not the debt service funds, thus a funding mechanism with no dedicated tax increase for Phase 1 of their plan. Figure 5.3 shows the front entrance of Northwood Middle School, in Highland Park, Illinois. The left shows the old view, and the right shows the modernization, improvement, and result of the new Long-Range Facilities Planning process.

This would show the community that the District would use taxes extended from the operations fund to repay the bonds over twenty years instead of automatically upping taxes on the community via a more traditional referendum bond issue. In addition, even if this first phase was all the district could accomplish, its equity lens of decision-making called for each child in every neighborhood to benefit from the middle school construction. All children attend middle school in the district. Even if they could not advance planning for a second phase, all children would still benefit from this transformative approach to the long-standing problems. This was proof of concept.

There are many leadership lessons in this story. One major, overarching lesson from this experience rests in the realm of community engagement and listening. Developing deep awareness and knowledge of others' viewpoints and perspectives involves the following details:

- Educational leaders create opportunities for sharing individual personal experiences and perspectives to develop awareness of and empathy for the feelings and thoughts of others.
- Educational leaders implement protocols that incorporate the elements of committed listening and effective, purposeful paraphrasing to demonstrate respect and support to build reciprocal trust among all stakeholders.
- Educational leaders collaboratively identify and implement processes that allow openness in the exploration of others' innovative ideas and perspectives.

Sheninger and Murray, in *Learning Transformed: 8 Keys to Designing Tomorrow's Schools, Today,* capture the spirit of going beyond community engagement to community collaboration. "In a traditional model of community engagement, districts will 'push' their content to the community and there will be little 'pull' in return. Community collaboration requires tactical push-pull balance." As educational leaders and authors, we seek input not only from our own practice and observations but from the leading writers and researchers of our time.

The survey also asked the community for input on the construction needs throughout the district's schools. The Long Range Facilities Committee had started meeting and ideas were being identified, focusing on construction. The District asked questions, held meetings, planned, asked again, and further and better refined their plans.

> The challenge that's being addressed: Participants are concerned about the potential impact of school closures and reconfigurations on the quality of education. They want to ensure that changes are made in the best interest of students' education.
>
> **Approach 1**: Prioritize student learning outcomes when making decisions about school closures and reconfigurations. This could involve

consulting with educational experts and reviewing research on the impact of school size and configuration on student learning

Approach 2: Regularly assess the quality of education at each school and make necessary adjustments to ensure high standards are maintained. This could include regular teacher evaluations, student assessments, and feedback from parents and students.

Approach 3: Provide ongoing professional development for teachers to help them adapt to changes and continue to deliver high-quality instruction.

The textbox above shows how even though finance and facilities were being analyzed and construction options were being considered, the focus was clarifying the education of children. Even though they were bringing closure to decades-long debates about configuration and buildings, the aim here was to make decisions that would impact student learning.

Educational leaders also support and implement practices that encourage an active flow of ideas. In *The Devil Is in the Details: System Solutions for Equity, Excellence, and Student Well-Being*, Fullan and Gallagher state, "Our conclusion is that deep sustainable change across a school system happens when staff at all levels experience leading learning together." They share seven similar and compatible leadership supports that create conditions for idea sharing:

1. Jointly determine focus on learning
2. Build coherence
3. Build collaborative culture
4. Recruit and build professional capacity
5. Differentiate support
6. Communicate and influence
7. Engage in inquiry

We put the "We're Not Broke, We're Broken" case study through the CHANGE framework upon which the book and its stories are built:

- *C—Challenge the Status Quo:* In the District 112 transformation, the status quo of failure was challenged vigorously through vision, leadership, community engagement, board governance, courage, and flexibility. Instead of complaining about the differing opinions, they sought out common ground. The new status quo was hope and accomplishment.

- *H—Have Open Conversations:* From the initial survey results, the follow-up committee meetings, and the open, public communication about the new approaches to a vexing and long-standing problem, it was all open, and it was all conversation. They shared meeting minutes, summaries, and videos so that the whole community could see what was being discussed. They listened and acted on the input. They changed approaches like refraining from selling park land at the request of the neighborhood requests.

- *A—Adapt and Be Flexible:* The revised approach from administration and board to community, administration, and board shows adaptive positions. The changed view from "one big fix" to multiple phases shows adaptive approaches and flexibility. They learned to slow down and be deliberate to get where they needed to go. They learned to be measured and reflective and to balance speed with accuracy.

- *N—Navigate Obstacles:* The district was fighting against recent history. The community norms around the district were anger and mistrust. Doing the work is a hard enough obstacle to overcome. The true obstacle was not only doing the work, but also doing it in a way that rebuilt trust with their stakeholders. There were obstacles that came up with the Long Range Plan, with curriculum and instruction and with the follow-up plans. They followed their playbook of leadership and overcame and navigated each obstacle with grace and success.

- *G—Generate a Shared Vision:* The shared vision came from the community: Equity, Instruction and Curriculum, Teachers and Staff, and Twenty-first-Century Facilities. With that guidance, it became the job of the leadership team to implement it. When there were issues from the community, they could always point back to the direction that was given to them by that same community. The shared vision of success, stability, excellence, fiscal responsibility, and guaranteed and viable curriculum drove their work.

- *E—Enjoy the Journey:* Through video, blog posts, emails, web news, community meetings in person, board presentations, it was clear that there was joy in the design, creation, and execution of the plan. This is indicative of the leadership journey we're all on. It's not an event. It's not one and done. It's fun to know what the community wants and get to actually do it! Seven years of organizational culture results, shown in Figure 2.3 illustrate one of the many metrics and data points of enjoying the journey in D112.

In summary, North Shore Elementary School District #112, faced significant turmoil leading up to Mike's appointment as superintendent in 2018. The district experienced instability with four acting superintendents over a short period of time, a failed $200+MM referendum in 2016, and widespread community dissatisfaction, resulting in leadership turnover and negative media coverage. The leadership team identified the district's core issue as a need to restore trust and stability.

As we contemplate the leadership lessons from the literature and from the case study highlighted, we revisit the reflective questions posed at the beginning:

- In what ways has community input shifted priorities and impacted your leadership?
- How do you look at historic decisions in your organization to help guide your future planning?
- How has strategic planning unified your community toward a shared purpose?
- What priorities and urgent needs exist in your organization right now?

In their book, *Leading Beautifully: Educational Leadership as Connoisseurship*, English and Ehrich (2016) argue that effective leadership goes beyond managing—leaders must approach their work as connoisseurs, blending innovation with a deep understanding of their community. The case study and successful leadership are illustrative of the new superintendent and Board of Education as connoisseurs of leadership. They demonstrate time after time an ability to meet the community's needs, to focus on student needs, and to repair and rehabilitate the image and perception of the District.

One of the ways educational leaders can support an active flow of ideas and creativity is expounded upon in their book, referring to the idea that there is no one answer. "There are no two days the same." The experiences in North

Shore School District 112 were certainly applicable to that quote—truly, no two days were the same!

Proven strategies, methods, and examples illustrate how to lead change successfully. It's incumbent upon us to lead for tomorrow's school today with as much support and collaboration as humanly possible. Through deliberate actions and community collaboration, the district successfully moved from a state of failure to one of renewed purpose and hope.

The leadership's commitment to equity, instructional quality, and modernizing facilities ensured that all students would benefit from the district's transformative approach. The district journey aligned its focus on what truly serves the best interests of its students and community, demonstrating the power of shared leadership and common purpose in overcoming challenges. Like the Kennedy quote at the start of the chapter, the story of recovery in District 112 illustrates that *Leadership and learning are indispensable to each other.*

6   **Transformation**
Flip the Mindset

Becoming is better than being.

—Carol Dweck

We love talking about a comic strip we came across a few years ago. The scene is a coffee shop where a caterpillar and a butterfly are sitting across from each other enjoying a drink. In the first panel, the caterpillar looks at the butterfly and says, "You've changed." In the next panel, the butterfly responds by saying, "We're supposed to!" It's been said that everyone wants change, but no one wants to change.

Futurist Jack Uldrich shares an interesting perspective on change and the idea of unlearning. Start by asking a roomful of people to imagine what two colors are included in a yield sign. After a moment, ask them to raise their hands if a yield sign is yellow and black. Many hands will shoot up throughout the room. You can then congratulate them on being correct—if that question was asked prior to 1971.

Ever since 1971, all yield signs in the United States have been red and white. So why do so many people answer yellow and black? The answer is that we, as humans, are really good at learning new information, but we are very bad at unlearning things that are no longer true. Unlearning is necessary in our personal and professional lives to clear out the old knowledge and make room for the new realities. In this chapter, we will explore how Leyden Community High School District 212 in Illinois flipped their mindset and did considerable unlearning.

Before diving into the case study, please take a moment to reflect on the following questions:

- Why is it so easy for us to learn but so hard for us to unlearn?
- In what ways can you shift from trying to become the best version of yourself to the next version of yourself?

- What takeaways do you hope to glean from this chapter to help create conditions for growth and learning in your organization?
- In what ways do you challenge your thinking and stretch your viewpoints so that you can help support and develop change?

In this chapter, the case study we share is from Leyden High School District 212 in suburban Chicago. Nick has served as the superintendent at Leyden for the past twelve years. Early in his tenure, he asked for teacher volunteers to be part of something they were calling the Innovation Incubator. It was an opportunity for teachers from a variety of content areas to come together and dream big about the next iteration of high school.

At Leyden, they created time for the teachers to meet and gave them no parameters. They literally had no idea what the teachers might come up with. In terms of flipping the script, the administration gave up the power and told the teachers to drive innovation. Like many great leaders, select the right people and then get out of their way!

As the teachers identified interesting programs across the state and across the country, they were allowed to travel and visit those schools and programs. One member of the Innovation Incubator even took a sabbatical year to travel and gather ideas both nationally and internationally.

While the team didn't find any program to copy, they found bits and pieces of ideas that eventually became a program that Leyden calls Co.Lab. Like we shared in Part II, Chapter 3, they went where the smart people were to learn more and apply that learning to their own setting.

Co.Lab is a reimagined version of the freshman year of high school, ninth grade. Traditionally, high school students move from classroom to classroom throughout each day. They spend 45–50 minutes learning about English, and then a bell rings. Next, they move to another classroom where they learn about science for 45–50 minutes until another bell rings. This pattern continues throughout the day, throughout the week, and throughout the years. The teachers behind Co.Lab asked, "What if we tried something different?" What if they flipped the mindset of what school looks like?

They proposed a four-period block of time where students would learn their subjects in an interdisciplinary fashion without passing periods. During that time, students would earn four and a half credits for digital literacy, English, health, physical education, science, and social studies. A dedicated team of teachers works with them every day. The various curricula are married together for project-based learning and standards-based grading.

The program was designed for students of all academic levels. There would be support for students with literacy or special education needs, and there would be an earned honors credit where the rubrics would allow for any student to work to the level of honors level grades.

Leyden caps participation to approximately 120 students per high school each year. Students opt-in to Co.Lab, or they can approach their freshman year in the traditional fashion. With that block of time each day, the teachers have a variety of options. They can get a bus and take the students to a local river to take water and ecological samples.

They can come back and analyze the sample or discuss the health impacts of water purification. They can assign a writing assignment or use social media to connect with their local legislators about protecting the local ecosystem. The possibilities are literally limitless.

Lessons can be conducted for whole groups, small groups, individuals, or a combination thereof. Co.Lab places a heavy emphasis on community involvement and advocacy. Each unit concludes with an exhibition where student learning is on display. Teachers, parents, and family members are invited into the school to see their work in person.

By design, the students work on their collaboration and public speaking skills. Now that Co.Lab has been in place for nearly ten years, teachers are reporting that former Co.Lab kids are different—in a good way. They want to get involved in their community. They thrive when working in collaboration with others, and they have higher levels of self-confidence in their work.

Before going into more detail, let's apply Leyden's Co.Lab program to the Satir Change Model:

- *Status Quo:* Prior to the transformation with Co.Lab, freshman year, ninth grade, at Leyden's high schools followed the traditional sequence of studies and organization of time. Students followed a bell schedule on the old factory model influenced by the nineteenth-century Prussian model. Teachers taught their unique (separate) content areas and operated in silos in relation to the teachers in the other content areas.

- *Foreign Element:* In this case, a dedicated, innovative, and creative group of teachers became the foreign element. They looked at the status quo and pushed back to say that things could be done differently. They were willing to put in the blood, sweat, and tears to create something new. Their aim was transformative leadership. The foreign element created Co.Lab.

- *Chaos:* As the group of teachers developed Co.Lab, many questions started surfacing. How would they plan for this high degree of collaboration and integration? How would they help eighth-grade students, parents, and teachers understand what this program was all about? There were questions from their peers in the department. There were questions from the teachers' union. Chaos was the uncertainty, the change, the different approaches, and the unknown outcomes.

- *Integration:* As the rollout of Co.Lab occurred, there were many questions about its efficacy and effectiveness. When the first batch of grade-level standardized tests was administered, many people watched with curiosity about what this new approach would garner in terms of assessment outcomes. There was a collective sigh of both relief and happiness when the results showed that students in Co.Lab performed as well or better than their classmates following the traditional pathway. Beyond standardized testing, there were speaking skill improvements, confidence skill improvements, and much, much, more. Co.Lab was becoming integrated into the core of Leyden.

- *New Status Quo:* Now, Co.Lab has been around for years. Older students are telling their younger siblings that they HAVE to do Co.Lab. Leyden has years with waiting lists where more students want to participate in the program than there are spaces available. In this new status quo, the current and former Co.Lab students are taking leadership positions in the school and throughout the community.

Ideally, as we explore and share in this book and in the field of leadership literature, a bit more time is generally far better for sustainable transformative change. This transformative program didn't happen overnight; it took years to develop the entirety of the program—and quite honestly, it continues to evolve every year.

The conditions that the superintendent, the Board of Education, and the leadership team established allowed for the teachers at Leyden to offer a flipped mindset version of freshman year. Because of that allowance to ideate and experiment, it has been able to flourish for many years.

In Carol Dweck's book *Mindset,* she calls upon us all to challenge our own assumptions about fixed and growth mindsets. She asserts that those with fixed mindsets give up easily and avoid change. Whereas, people with growth mindsets embrace change and challenges. In addition to Dweck's work on mindsets and psychology, diving into one's global mindset can also help to open one's mind. The quote at the start of this chapter, from Dweck, illustrates that belief.

Flipping one's mindset calls for knowing and understanding others. For example, collaborative leadership is a management practice in which members of a leadership team work together across sectors to make decisions and keep their organization thriving. Collaboration in an organization is an essential element for any change, and change is supported in an open-minded and "mindset-shifting" place. We're suggesting that mindset-flipping organizations are also those that embody a global mindset.

Throughout the book, we are demonstrating where and how generative artificial intelligence tools can be used to support learning, thinking, growing, and writing. In this context, and for this chapter. First, we asked Copilot, an artificial intelligence support tool from Microsoft, "What can you find out about the change experience at the Leyden High Schools in Illinois called Co.Lab?"

Here is what Copilot produced:

> The Co.Lab program at Leyden High Schools in Franklin Park, IL, is an innovative initiative designed to foster collaboration and provide a project-based learning experience for students. Here are some key aspects of the Co.Lab experience:
>
> **1.** *Interdisciplinary Curriculum: The Co.Lab program integrates subjects such as English, biology, global studies, health, and digital literacy. This interdisciplinary approach helps students see the connections between different fields of study and apply their knowledge in a more holistic way.*

2. *Design Thinking Process: The program uses a design thinking process to encourage creativity and problem-solving. This method helps students develop critical thinking skills and approach challenges with a solution-oriented mindset.*
3. *Technology Integration: Classrooms are equipped with wall-mounted video monitors and group seating arrangements to facilitate collaboration. Students can easily share their screens and work together on projects, enhancing their digital literacy and teamwork skills.*
4. *Community and Identity Themes: The curriculum is designed to connect students' studies to themes such as identity, community, and wellness. This helps make learning more relevant and engaging for students.*
5. *Support During Remote Learning: Even during the Covid-19 pandemic, the Co.Lab program maintained low failure rates, thanks to its strong sense of community and deliberate empowerment of students.*
6. *Exhibition of Work: At the end of the year, students participate in an exhibition to showcase the projects they have worked on throughout the year. This provides a sense of accomplishment and allows students to share their learning with the broader community.*

The Co.Lab program at Leyden High Schools represents a significant shift toward personalized and interdisciplinary education, aiming to better prepare students for the complexities of the modern world.

Next, we asked another artificial intelligence tool, Magic School AI, to summarize a YouTube video about this Co.Lab, and here is that summary:

Summary of Co.Lab Interdisciplinary Program

The Co.Lab interdisciplinary program is offered at West Leyden and East Leyden for freshmen across periods three through nine. It integrates subjects such as biology, global studies, English, digital literacy, physical education, and health. The program was developed by a dedicated group of educators with the goal of creating a new educational experience at the high school level. The main objective is to ignite passion and maintain student engagement by connecting various curriculums.

During the four-hour program, students engage in activities across different subjects all working towards a common goal. Co.Lab emphasizes project-based learning, hands-on experiences, and collaboration rather than traditional tests. Students have the opportunity to continuously revise and improve until they master the required skills.

One of the key features of Co.Lab is its focus on student empowerment and community engagement. Each quarter, students showcase their knowledge through artifacts and projects, enhancing their leadership skills. The program themes guide students to explore topics and projects of their interest, promoting essential skills like discussion and collaboration.

Co.Lab is best suited for students who are eager to challenge themselves, take initiative in their own learning, build strong relationships, enhance confidence, and drive positive change within their community. Participants benefit from developing design principles, communication skills, and leadership attributes, enabling them to pursue their passions and voice their opinions effectively. Overall, Co.Lab helps students grow personally, academically, and socially, fostering maturity and confidence.

As shared in the summary, the organization, the conditions for learning, and the overall experience show a flipped mindset and a change to open-mindedness. The Co.Lab experience is emblematic of a leadership culture where "why not" is emphasized over "why." It needs to become the norm for us to continue to create conditions for the future of our students. They are living in exponential times, and we must lead exponentially.

In addition to examples like the one above, an exponential growth mindset can be sustained and nurtured through a modern view of professional learning and development.

Let's look at how this flipped mindset and transformational change to ninth grade can be analyzed through the utilization of the CHANGE Leadership Framework:

- **C—Challenge the Status Quo:** This group of Leyden teachers was willing to think differently and put in the time and effort to build something new. They traveled to see what was happening in other places, and they used that knowledge to pick and choose aspects of what would work in their schools, in their community, and for their kids. They knew there would be opposition, so it was imperative that the administration provide them with the resources they needed, and more importantly, the administration provided them with the time and support they needed to make their ideas a reality. They literally challenged the status quo of how freshman year, ninth grade, was designed, implemented, and experienced.

- *H—Have Open Conversations:* Some of the original Innovation Incubator teachers opted not to persist and become part of the Co.Lab team. They returned to the traditional format of teaching, and that was okay. The teachers themselves advocated for the need for a common release period to plan and coordinate for this unique program. They built talking points to recruit students and families to this program before it even actually existed. There was honest, authentic feedback and two-way communication throughout the process of discovery and exploration.

- *A—Adapt and Be Flexible:* The administration had to be flexible to allow for the development of a unique approach to educate ninth-grade students. The teachers were clearly adapting their work to try something new for their students. Finally, the teachers' union had to adapt to the fact that this group of teachers was receiving an additional collaborative prep period in order to support this unique approach to collaborative teaching. There is flexibility inherent in the dual approaches to freshman year. There is flexibility in Co.Lab coexisting with the traditional approach.

- *N—Navigate Obstacles:* As Co.Lab became a reality, there were a lot of critics immediately. Some elementary schools questioned whether this program was for advanced students or struggling students. (Of course, it was designed for *all* students.) Teachers who taught the traditional form of the included courses questioned whether or not Co.Lab could possibly teach students all of the necessary material that was being taught in the year-long, standalone courses. Other obstacles came up during the equality/equity debates. Should ninth grade be the same for everyone, or should there be options that meet the needs of the greatest number of students?

- *G—Generate a Shared Vision:* In this case, that group of teachers, with the support of their administration, generated a shared vision of what

Co.Lab could be. As time has passed, two things have happened. Upper-level teachers have seen the effect of students taking part in Co.Lab and bringing a higher level of collaborative and self-confidence skills. And time has cemented this program as part of the school culture. The vision is also shared with the students and their families.

- *E—Enjoy the Journey:* The district has hosted visits and allowed other teachers to come and see how Co.Lab was built and how it operates. They have also allowed the teaching staff to share their story at state and national conferences. The biggest enjoyment comes from attending the exhibitions that the students host every year so that all can see their learning and the joy they have in what they do and create.

Before we bring this chapter to a close, please take some reflection time with the reflection questions from this chapter, first introduced at the beginning of the chapter,

- Why is it so easy for us to learn but so hard for us to unlearn?
- In what ways can you shift from trying to become the best version of yourself to the next version of yourself?
- What takeaways do you hope to glean from this chapter and this book to help create conditions for growth and learning in your organization?
- In what ways do you challenge your thinking and stretch your viewpoints so that you can help support and develop change?

Co.Lab was the right program at the right time for the students and community at Leyden. That doesn't mean it's the right thing for your district—but that's not the point. The real point is that we all need to challenge the way we have always done things. The world is changing faster than we can comprehend.

We can either do everything we can to change to keep up with the pace of the world our kids live in, or we can risk becoming quickly irrelevant as an institution. Leading for tomorrow's schools today almost demands a mindset change so that the future for our students is the focus—the windshield, not the rearview mirror.

Change requires courage and trust. If you foster the right conditions and empower your teams, there is no limit to what they can achieve. So, we ask you, who in your organization is ready to make the leap? Who is waiting to be part of your Innovation Incubator? What innovation will they come up with? And, finally, do you have the will and the trust to support them as they create a new reality for your students?

Voices from the Field
Expanding Pathways to Success

Gladys I. Cruz

Background

The high school experience today varies greatly across our nation's schools in terms of minimum graduation requirements, diploma options, assessments, and pathways to advancement.[1]

In terms of the main coursework, the picture is somewhat different given that the courses required for graduation across many schools throughout the nation continue to reflect the recommendations of The Report of the Committee of Ten in 1892.[2] Charles W. Eliot, president of Harvard University at that time, led a group tasked with determining the high school program of studies and the college admission requirements. Over 133 years later, we still find the program of studies in many high schools across our nation aligned with the recommendations of the Committee of Ten. (See Table 6B.1.)

It is important to point out that the recommendations of 1892 included four years of study in each of the basic disciplines of English, mathematics, foreign languages, sciences, and history—a trend that is still valued in today's institutions of higher education. This course of studies and similar programs of study today are mainly college preparatory programs, although dramatic changes in today's technological advances, the economy, and the changing Pre-K–12 student population call for a different course of preparation and pathways to prepare students for their futures.

Why Change

At the heart of the debate of why change today's public high school experience is the question: What is the purpose of public education? Depending on whom we ask, the answer to this question can take us down

Table 6B.1 Committee of Ten HS Recommended Courses of Study of 1892

Ninth Grade (First Secondary School Year)	Tenth Grade (Second Secondary School Year)
• Latin • English Literature • English Composition • German or French • Algebra • History	• Latin • Greek • English Literature • English Composition • German • French • Algebra • Geometry • Astronomy • Botany or Zoology • History
Eleventh Grade (Third Secondary School Year)	Twelfth Grade (Fourth Secondary School Year)
• Latin • Greek • English Literature • English Composition • Rhetoric • German • French • Algebra • Geometry • Chemistry • History	• Latin • Greek • English Literature • English Composition • English Grammar • German • French • Trigonometry • Higher Algebra • Physics • Anatomy, Physiology, and Hygiene • History • Geology or Physiography • Meteorology

Source: James C. Mackenzie, "The Report of the Committee of Ten," *The School Review*, Vol. 2, No. 3 (Mar., 1894), pp. 146–155. Published by: The University of Chicago Press.

different paths regarding the purpose of education, how it would impact curricular content and students' educational experiences, and who should decide what the curricular and educational content should be. On the matter of public education's purpose, a Phi Delta Kappa's (PDK's) 2016 poll on the public's attitudes toward public education[3] revealed there was no consensus on what the objectives of education should be. Some respondents (45 percent) believed that academic achievement was the main goal, while preparing students for the workforce and citizenry were identified by roughly 25 percent of respondents. Interestingly, as they addressed questions of educational content and experiences, 68 percent of respondents to this same poll indicated that they would prefer schools to focus more on career/technical skills over honors or advanced academic classes. As for who should decide what to teach, in a more recent PDK 2023 poll,[4] a wide majority of respondents (66 percent) indicated that teachers should have a say in the courses that are taught at high schools, at a higher level than policy makers or boards of education.

It is true that public school systems' values and priorities reflect their local, regional, and state contexts, infusing a great deal of diversity in the K–12 experience and goals across contexts. At the same time, the reasons why public schools came into being—preparing people for jobs and citizenship, unifying a diverse population, and promoting equity, among others—remain relevant, even urgent, today across the public school system. While the debate on what this looks like in terms of curricular design and educational practice is long from finalized, there is an emerging consensus on the need to ensure a high-quality education that offers students choices so that the purposes of education are met.

In the report *K–12 Education: Transforming Public Education for a Changing World*, The Center for American Progress[5] documents the following six policy proposals to transform the P-12 school system:

1. Supporting a well-prepared, valued, and skilled workforce;
2. Modernizing school facilities;
3. Ensuring equitable and ethical uses of AI and education technologies;
4. Supporting the whole child approach to education;
5. Strengthening and expanding high-quality college and career pathways; and
6. Providing adequate and equitable student funding ensures students meet the demands of a changing world.

All these broad proposals are critical and need to be actualized by means of specific practices to transform P–12 systems and redefine what a quality education looks like for all students. I will focus in this chapter mainly on the ideals of proposal 5, *strengthening and expanding high-quality college and career pathways*.

A Quality Education Redefined

How we define a quality education and for whom are also questions educators will continue to grapple with for the foreseeable future. Is quality of education defined by a ranking on an international, national, or state test? Is it defined by the number of students who graduate? Is it the number of students that go on to post-secondary education? Should it be redefined by technical programs addressing the needs of the trades and the workplace ensuring that our economy continues to flourish? Should it be defined as how well we prepare students for post-secondary education, ensuring that our colleges and universities continue to remain relevant? Should it be by preparing the populace to become active and engaged citizens, ensuring that our democracy continues to exist? Or should it be on how well we prepare young people to enter the different branches of the armed services?

I would argue that we must redefine the quality of education via different criteria that offer diverse and different pathways to meet the needs and abilities of all learners while ensuring that our workforce demands are met, our economy continues to flourish, and our democracy continues to exist as we know it. In the book *Other Ways to Win: Creating Alternatives for High School Graduates*,[6] Kenneth Gray and Edwin Herr discuss that we need to move away from the notion that the only way to be successful after high school is to go to college. They indicate that while everyone in the United States can have access and enter post-secondary education programs, it is a myth that college graduates will have a job upon completion of their degrees that is commensurate with their studies. They assert as the title suggests and I agree that there are other ways to win.

The Case for Multiple Pathways

In 2021, the McKinsey Group[7] published a report indicating that the future workforce will require a different set of skills. The McKinsey Group identified four broad skill categories and thirteen sub-skill sets within these categories for a total of fifty-six skill sets or Deltas. These include *cognitive*—critical thinking, planning and ways of working, communication, and mental flexibility; *interpersonal*—mobilizing systems, developing relationships, and teamwork effectiveness; *digital*—digital fluency and citizenship, software use and development, and understanding digital systems; and *self-leadership*—self-awareness and self-management, entrepreneurship, and goals achievement. In defining these skills, the McKinsey Group supports the fact that some work will require a level of specialization and higher education; however, they stress that citizens will need a set of foundational skills that help them fulfill the following three criteria, no matter the sector in which they work or their occupation:

- Add value beyond what can be done by automated systems and intelligent machines;
- Operate in a digital environment;
- Continually adapt to new ways of working and new occupations.

These criteria challenge us to expand our educational programs and pathways for students, ensuring we align them to the workforce and the ever-changing technologies. Questar III BOCES, a Board of Cooperative Educational Services serving twenty-two school districts in Rensselaer, Columbia, and Greene counties in upstate New York, offers a variety of programs providing students of all ages, abilities, backgrounds, and interests an opportunity to broaden their educational horizons by attending a variety of innovative programs that lead to many pathways. We offer a world-class high school education program through two comprehensive STEM high schools located on college campuses. One of these schools—Tech Valley High School[8] is a partnership with Capital Region BOCES, expanding opportunities to students in various counties in Albany's Capital Region. This school is located on the State University at Albany campus. The second is STEM High School[9] located at Hudson Valley Community College. Questar III BOCES also offers two-year programs in fifteen trades at two state-of-the-art technical schools and seven New Visions seniors-only programs at colleges, universities, an arts center, a hospital, and other sites that become the classroom for exciting and innovative programs. All these learning opportunities offer a myriad of future pathways for secondary school students.

Tech Valley High School

Tech Valley High School (TVHS)—a regional comprehensive high school—offers a college preparatory program with opportunities for students to discover their passions well beyond post-secondary education. The school is a project-based school and a member of the New Tech Network (NTN)[10] of Schools, located on the College of Nanotechnology, Science, and Engineering campus at the University at Albany. Students learn their content mainly through project-based learning. TVHS students work in teams and collaborate to solve problems that are often pitched by local businesses or impact their community. Students present their findings to an audience of experts and are evaluated with the use of a rubric. Students are evaluated on more than just content. This school includes agency and self-direction, collaboration, communication, knowing and thinking, and technology and information as the school-wide learning outcomes, and receive grades in these areas. A school with a 100 percent graduation rate since its inception—the school is truly a different high school. From interdisciplinary courses taught through project-based learning (PBL) to I-Terms, which are out-of-school learning experiences where students explore their passions or the fields they think they would like to pursue. Students can receive an associate degree if they wish to enhance their post-secondary opportunities.

An element that separates this school from many traditional high schools, in addition to the wall-to-wall project-based learning, is what the school calls the I-Term. This is where students can spend up to two weeks exploring the intersection of their passions and career pathways using the concept of Ikigai—a Japanese term that blends "iki," which means to live, and "gai" which translates to "a reason for being." TVHS students use a simple diagram with four intersecting circles representing passion: what we love; mission: what the world needs; vocation: what you can get paid for; and profession: what you are good at. Students have completed their I-Terms in wide-ranging locations such as the FBI, New York State Governor's Office, Wadsworth Center of the New York State Health Department, and American Cancer Society.

STEM High School

STEM High School is a partnership between Hudson Valley Community College and Questar III BOCES to offer an innovative high school merging an Early College High School and a P-TECH High School to benefit the diverse student populations seeking various pathways within the overarching areas of Computer Information Systems, Engineering Technology, Environmental

Science, and Health Sciences. STEM High School students learn through project-based inquiry approaches. In addition to being housed in a building totally integrated within the College, students have the entire college campus as their "school." Students begin taking college courses integrated with college students as early as freshman year. The school opened its doors during the pandemic. Three years later, some students have already completed their high school requirements and a two-year college degree in one of the four STEM pathways offered by the school.

An element that separates this high school from traditional high schools is the close partnership with the college, allowing students to have the college campus as their "school" and be fully integrated with college students in classes on the college campus.

Career and Technical Education (CTE) Programs

There has been growing support across the nation for CTE programs. CTE programs can serve as a bridge to workforce stability. Skilled trade vacancies have been the hardest to fill in the United States for several years. According to the US Bureau of Labor Statistics, many of the skilled occupations have median ages above forty-five, which underscores the importance of preparing a new pipeline of skilled workers.

Questar III BOCES offers fifteen trade programs in our technical schools offering students a "hands-on experience" in trades coupled with the latest technologies, including industry-grade simulators coupled with college credits. These programs develop students' skills in many areas identified by the McKinsey Group.

The CTE programs are two-year half-day high school programs in a variety of trades that are aligned to the workforce in high-paying careers, preparing students to enter the workforce, higher education, or the armed services right out of high school.

The CTE programs range from aviation, gaming, pathways in education, to heavy equipment operations and maintenance, agriculture, to more common programs such as welding and metal fabrication, HVAC, cosmetology, or culinary arts.

These programs provide students with integrated academics in language arts, science, and mathematics giving students opportunities to apply these subjects in their fields of study where they can better understand the "why" they need to understand the concepts and processes. Students in our CTE programs have excelled at both state and national competitions, earning awards and scholarships. Programs have also earned excellence awards, and most recently, the Robert H. Gibson Technical School was recognized as one of SkillsUSA's Models of Excellence nationally. It is the highest honor bestowed on chapters of SkillsUSA.

Graduation rates of students attending CTE programs are steadily in the upper 1990s and we pride ourselves in our graduates achieving high rates of technical endorsement in their trades. All our programs benefit from direct connections with experts in the trades through trade advisory committees that meet with our instructors and provide feedback on the curriculum, equipment, and technologies used in the field.

A special feature of our CTE programs is our Youth Apprenticeship Program, where students participate in paid internships or apprenticeships in over thirty businesses in the region. Our BOCES is the only BOCES in NYS partnering with businesses to offer youth apprenticeships to our CTE students.

New Visions Programs

The New Visions programs are one-year high school to college bridge programs. These programs are intended for high-achieving seniors that are pretty much done with high school and are looking for a challenge. This includes the valedictorians and salutatorians from some of our local high schools. Questar III BOCES offers seven innovative New Visions programs in diverse areas ranging from business, finance, and marketing located on a community college campus, to a medical program housed in a hospital, to an Emergency Preparedness, Informatics, Cyber and Homeland Security (EPICH) program located at the University at Albany's ETEC, a 246,000 square foot state-of-the-art building that "houses" researchers, educators, and entrepreneurs, to a Visual and Performing Arts program located at a local arts center. These programs offer "hands-on" project-based learning experiences such as hospital rotations, business plan development, and the creation of special projects in all facets of the program of studies coupled with college credits. These programs prepare students to pursue post-secondary studies in many fields of study. Students in New Visions programs fine-tune their critical thinking skills, oral and written communication skills, creativity, innovation, collaboration, problem-solving, cultural literacy, and interpersonal skills throughout this one-year, seniors-only experience.

Students attending the CTE and New Visions programs have opportunities to enter over 170 fields or potential careers. CTE students can also achieve over one-hundred industry certifications within their fields of study. This includes an FAA Private Pilot License, UAS Drone Certification, Occupational Safety and Health Administration (OSHA) Safety Certification, New York State Certified Health Assistant Certification, American Heart Association CPR Certification for Healthcare Provider, Environmental Protection Agency (EPA) 608 Certification, GasTite CSST Certification, Dig Safely New York, Inc. Certified Excavator Program, New York State Department of Health EMT-B Certification, New York State Basic Exterior Firefighting Operations with Hazardous Material First Responder Operation, ServSafe® Food Safety Certification, New York State Restaurant Association Educational Foundation Culinary Arts Certification, New York State Cosmetologist License, SP2 National Safety Certification, and the National Institute for Automotive Service Excellence (ASE) Student Certification in Maintenance & Light Repair, among many others.

Concluding Thoughts

As groups and states look to redefine and modernize coursework and graduation requirements, it is important to continue to reflect on the purpose of education in preparing diverse students of all ages and abilities. Hands-on programs that bridge the gap between theory and practice, fostering a deeper understanding of learning, are critical in preparing students for the realities of the real world. BOCES programs like STEM comprehensive high schools, CTE, and New Visions programs empower students to explore different career paths and build sought-after skills in the job market as well as for college. As the world continues to evolve, hands-on learning that continues to be aligned with changing technologies will remain an essential tool for preparing students to thrive in an increasingly dynamic environment, one where they will need to continue to learn and adapt.

Notes

1. Ben Erwin, Daizha Brown, and Sharmila Mann, 50 State Comparison, Education Commission of the States, see complete state profiles at http://ecs.force.com/mbdata/mbprofall?Rep=HS01.

2. James C. Mackenzie, "The Report of the Committee of Ten," *The School Review*, Vol. 2, No. 3 (Mar., 1894), pp. 146–155. Published by: The University of Chicago Press.

3. Tim Walker, "NEA Today: What's the Purpose of Education? Public Doesn't Agree on the Answer," https://www.nea.org/nea-today/all-news-articles/whats-purpose-education-public-doesnt-agree-answer (August 29, 2026).

4. PDK Poll on the Public's Attitudes towards Public Schools, The 55th Annual PDK Poll https://pdkpoll.org/2023-pdk-poll-results/

5. Waede James, Building an Economy for All, K–12 Education: Transforming Public Education for a Changing World, Center for American Progress (November 4, 2024). K–12 Education: Transforming Public Education for a Changing World—Center for American Progress.

6. Kenneth C. Gray, and Edwin L. Herr (Eds.), *Other Ways to Win: Creating Alternatives for High School Graduates*, 3rd Edition. Corwin.

7. Marco Dondi, Julia Klier, Fríedéric Panier, and Jörg Schubert, "Defining the Skills that Citizens will Need for the Future of Work," McKinsey and Company, June 25, 2021, https://www.mckinsey.com/industries/public-sector/our-insights/defining-the-skills-citizens-will-need-in-the-future-world-of-work

8. New Tech Network https://newtechnetwork.org/

9. Tech Valley High School https://www.techvalleyhigh.org/

10. STEM HS https://www.questar.org/education/ptech-echs/

Part IV
Change Faster—Embrace Your Context—Revolutionary Change

7 Bomb Threats and Social Media

You can have brilliant ideas, but if you can't get them across, your ideas won't get you anywhere.

—Lee Iacocca

Since 2010, we have been evangelizing the value of using social media tools for communication in leadership. We founded and ran an international chat on Twitter (X) called #suptchat for 10 years, hosting 100 episodes. We have presented locally, regionally, statewide, nationally, and internationally on the value of social media for communications, especially for leaders.

Our district hashtags were known widely: #LeydenPride, #Engage109, and #112Leads. We've written about Twitter (X), Voxer, blogging, video, podcasting, and more! Most importantly, we amplify messages of good to reframe the narrative of public education. We tell our stories so someone else does not have to.

In this chapter, we explore the complete transformation of communication approaches in North Shore School District 112 due to external threats. You will read how Mike and his team went from "all in" on district communications using social media, featuring daily images of children and staff, to an abrupt and complete shutdown and prohibition of all public imagery of students or staff. Five years of successful practices shifted overnight due to threats and new realities.

As you read through this chapter, we ask you to reflect on the following questions:

- What does telling your own story mean to you?
- How might you improve your communication approaches, and why?
- Are there instances where you reveal agility in leadership by changing successful practices due to situations that call those practices into question?
- When should community input cause you to change course for yourself and the district?

In District 112, on July 1, 2018, Mike and his team presented the new hashtag #112Leads to signify a new era in the school district. All were part of the leadership and the new journey! As you read in Chapter 5, the district was in dire need of a redo. #112Leads and the strategic use of communication to change their narrative were foundational to the leadership playbook in use in District 112 from July 1, 2018, through September/November 2023.

With respect to communication and the approaches with social media, leadership believed that everything was going well, until, well, it wasn't! The superintendent's playbook needed a change. This is the story of #112Leads and how multiple non-credible bomb threats and social media attacks led to a total transformation of communication approaches in eight weeks.

In leadership, you learn that "stuff happens." And in September 2023, in North Shore School District 112 in Highland Park, Illinois, the stuff hit the fan. Leading for tomorrow's schools today calls on leaders to be nimble, agile, compassionate, and responsive. North Shore School District 112 became the victim of swatting. Swatting is the act of reporting fake threats to emergency responders, intentionally triggering a large law enforcement response. Many industries, including K–12 schools, have repeatedly fallen victim to these calls. These false threats divert precious resources and create room for real dangers.

For instance:

- In just one month in 2023, at least 210 swatting threats were made against K–12 schools.
- According to the Anti-Defamation League (ADL), there were at least 1,000 swatting incidents in 2019. A 2023 ADL survey found that 11 percent of teens and 5 percent of adults reported experiencing swatting in their lifetime.
- Specifically regarding K–12 schools, in 2023, there were at least 723 swatting hoaxes, according to the K–12 School Shooting Database.

In September 2023, a series of three non-credible bomb threats (swatting) at one of the schools in the district caused great distress at the school and in the community. The non-credible bomb threats can be tied to attacks on social media against the school, staff, and administration based on perceived offensive content. The previous five years of communication strategies and social media proliferation were immediately questioned and vigorously challenged. If ever there was a need for a leadership lesson and intervention, it was then. The three bomb threats took place over a five day period.

Regardless of the actual cause or intent, each bomb threat was non-credible. The leadership lesson here is that even successful leadership strategies can be called into question, and leaders who lead for tomorrow's schools today demonstrate adaptability and agility. While it was not directly proven that social media attacks led to the threats, there was enough circumstantial evidence and occurrences like this around the nation, that change was demanded by the community, and heeded by the leadership.

To better understand the transformation, we can apply the Satir Change Model to the district's experience. As we share in each chapter, the Satir Change Model outlines five stages of organizational change: Status Quo, Foreign Element, Chaos, Integration, and New Status Quo. Applying this model to District 112's experience can provide deeper insights. The district navigated from chaos to a new status quo during this very public, very tense, and relatively fast time frame, marking an inflection moment for the district and its leadership.

- *Status Quo:* July 1, 2018, to November 2023, the district was using student images and various social media platforms like Twitter (X), LinkedIn, Facebook, Instagram, and others on a daily basis. This was the norm, the reality, even the expectation, for the better part of five consecutive years as part of their broader communication strategy. That use of social media was a pride point for the district and a regular part of their daily business.

- *Foreign Element:* After the three non-credible bomb threats over five days in September 2023, the community perceived direct safety risks connected to social media. There were multiple attacks on social media (thousands of likes and reposts). The experience was both educational and disruptive. Bomb threats, in and of themselves, cause chaos for a minute. The rest of the community and the staff also strongly questioned the continued usage of social media tools for the district, especially images of students and staff in public forums. The swatting, social media attacks, and bomb threats were foreign elements.

- *Chaos:* Immediate and intense calls for change in communication and social media were coming from one school and then from the entire district. Frustration and fear was evident and calls for change grew fast. Social media was a huge part of the traditions and norms of the schools and community. This conversation turned all of that upside down. The officials had to address and deal with the bomb threats. They were working with first responders, multiple agency detection dogs and other investigation tools. Their primary concern and motivation was student, staff, and facility safety. They also had to deal with the fear, anxiety, fallout, and demands for change from a jolted community. This is a community that endured the tragic July 4, 2022, mass shooting; nerves were frayed and folks were on edge.

- *Integration:* The district leadership, through immediate community engagement and reflection, integrated the communication aims and the community input. One outreach survey was administered on a Sunday (after two of the non-credible bomb threats the previous Thursday and Friday). Based on listening, analysis, and change leadership, the district made an immediate and complete shift in terms of communication and public sharing. They moved to a non-public, walled approach to sharing information among their stakeholders. They kept true to their philosophy and core values of sharing the success and powerful stories of education—just now, these images are in a walled, secure access format called Parent Square. They went from open source, public social media to a total and abrupt prohibition of any images of individuals in public forums.

- *New Status Quo:* In this new reality, the school district is still reaching their stakeholders, sharing good news, and communicating necessary information. But they are doing it in a more private way in accordance with the current wishes of everyone involved. What started as a crisis, ended as a collaborative win. The new status quo enhanced and reaffirmed the public trust in the administration and board. The new status quo encouraged more parents to use the walled garden communication tools and the new status quo removed a number of risks, real, perceived, and experienced.

The district demonstrated adaptive change management by soliciting feedback from parents, staff, the Board of Education, and other community partners, revealing significant discontent and leading to the chaos described above. Through thoughtful review of purpose, practice and aims, continuous improvement, and a new inspired shared vision, the district successfully established a new communication approach, gaining community support and appreciation. The leadership kept its core values of authenticity, transparency, and direct communication. They simply pivoted from public to private.

The leadership illustrated continuous improvement and openness to change. Feedback, input, and planning took place, leading to a significant challenge to the process after five consecutive years of prolific communication and image sharing. See Table 7.1 for the internal SWOT (Strengths, Weaknesses, Opportunities, and Threats) Analysis of the District's Approach to Social Media Use for Communication. This SWOT was developed and created via a third-party software partner called Thought Exchange. It was created based upon community input and feedback in an online survey. In the figure, strengths and weaknesses were identified, including the following key takeaways,

- Strengths:
  - Some participants appreciate the sense of connection and community.
  - Real-time updates can be beneficial.
- Weaknesses:
  - Discomfort with public sharing of videos and photos of students.
  - Opt-out policy for social media sharing needs review and clarification.
- Opportunities:
  - Use a more secure, private system.
  - Enhance privacy and focus on security.
- Threats:
  - Public images can be misused or turned into threats to student safety.
  - Potential legal issues related to privacy and consent.

Generative artificial intelligence (Gen AI) is part of the algorithm that the survey partner uses to generate the SWOT analysis shown in Table 7.1. The use of Gen AI is overt, embedded in sources and partners, and is becoming increasingly more prevalent in all facets of our world.

Table 7.1 SWOT Analysis

SWOT Analysis of District's Approach to Social Media Use for Communication	
This analysis is based on the feedback from participants regarding the district's current approach to using social media for communication, particularly the sharing of photos and videos of students and school activities.	
Strength	**Weakness**
Summary: The district's use of social media allows for real-time updates and a sense of community. It provides a platform to showcase the district's culture, activities, and achievements. **Key Takeaways:** • Some participants appreciate the sense of connection and community fostered by social media use. • Real-time updates can be beneficial for keeping parents informed.	**Summary:** The current approach to social media use has raise significant privacy and safety concerns among participants. The opt-out policy for social media sharing is seen as confusing and ineffective. **Key Takeaways:** • Many participants are uncomfortable with the public sharing of photos and videos of students. • The opt-out policy for social media sharing may need to be reviewed and communicated more clearly.
Opportunities	**Threats**
Summary: The district has the opportunity to review and revise its social media policies to address privacy and safety concerns. There is potential to explore more secure, private channels of communication. **Key Takeaways:** • Participants expressed a preference for more secure, private communication channels such as email, newsletters, and school-specific platforms. • There is a call for more stringent privacy measures and active parental consent.	**Summary:** The district's current use of social media could potentially expose students and staff to risks, including misuse of image, threats to safety, and potential legal issues. **Key Takeaways:** • Public sharing of photos and videos could potentially be misused or lead co threats to student safety. • There are potential legal implication related to privacy and consent.

Source: From North Shore School District 112.

Part of the journey is leading as a learner, leading as a student, and leading as a listener. The opportunities in the analysis allowed for the district to illustrate the leadership process and demonstrate leadership capacity. The opportunities proved to offer a new pathway forward. It's the journey that matters, not the event. Recall the quote at the start of Chapter 5 from John F. Kennedy, *Leadership and learning are indispensable to each other.* The execution of change shown in this case study is also an embodiment of that quote. The quote from this chapter from Lee Iacocca, *You can have brilliant ideas, but if you can't get them across, your ideas won't get you anywhere,* resonates with the entire case study. No ideas are actually brilliant if no one knows or can access those ideas.

As a result of the experiences in September, with great public input, open and public discussion, and flexible change, they immediately started to use a more secure, private system and they enhanced the privacy and security for students and staff alike. The district took a very negative set of events and turned it into an opportunity to build trust and partnership.

In Figure 7.1, we share the survey prompt which helped to lead to change, they were asking directly, what should we start, stop, or do more/less of? The prompt, shown in the image, asked the public to reflect on the district's approaches to social media use; they sought input on what should be started, stopped or increased. They listened and they acted.

Reading about this story in highlight form makes it look easy. It was not! Reading about it in highlight form makes it look like five years of one practice turned on its head overnight and made complete and total sense. It kind of did! The culture established in the organization had shown flexibility, agility, and open-mindedness over the preceding years. Even though no one ever really discussed the communication strategies, the events of September 2023 forced an accelerated change.

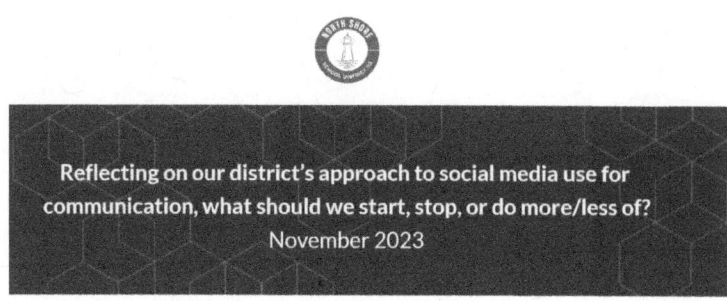

Figure 7.1 Survey prompt. *Source:* Michael Lubelfeld.

As you can see from Figure 7.2, the engagement was quite high with more than 900 participants giving input with nearly 700 unique thoughts.

Figure 7.3 shows that the pro-social media respondents and the anti-social media respondents reached common ground. The common ground consensus was that private platforms were OK, but public sharing of images was no longer acceptable. Like the SWOT analysis shown in Table 7.1, the common ground assessment shared in Figure 7.3 Common Ground from Survey, is generated by the Gen AI algorithms in Thought Exchange.

Both sides agreed on the need for effective communication. They agreed on the common ground of a secure, private platform to host their communication

Engagement

Review your current engagement statistics to understand how engaged participants are on this topic.

👤 Participants	💬 Thoughts	⭐ Ratings
909	677	17,024
Last activity: 30+ days ago	0.7 thoughts / participant	18.7 ratings / participant

Figure 7.2 Engagement survey. *Source:* Michael Lubelfeld.

Balancing Social Media Use

Side A — **Pro-Social Media**

Supporters of social media use in the district argue that it helps build a sense of community, allows parents to stay informed about school activities, and showcases the district's culture and achievements. They appreciate seeing photos and updates about their children and believe that social media is a critical tool for communication in today's world. Some suggest using private or closed groups to enhance safety while still sharing information.

Common ground — **Private Platforms**

Both sides agree on the importance of safety and privacy. A common ground is the use of private or closed platforms for sharing information and photos. This approach can satisfy the need for communication and community building while addressing concerns about public exposure and security risks. Ensuring that only verified parents and guardians have access to these platforms can help protect students and staff.

Side B — **Anti-Social Media**

Opponents of social media use in the district express concerns about privacy, safety, and the potential misuse of photos and information. They argue that public social media posts can expose students and staff to risks, including data harvesting and security threats. Many prefer alternative communication methods like email, newsletters, or private platforms that restrict access to only parents and guardians.

Figure 7.3 Common ground from survey. Illustration by Michael Lubelfeld.

systems. Those opposing viewpoints were used to unite the community on a complex issue by taking the time to listen, analyze, think, seek common ground, reframe goals and actions; and to change.

As you know, throughout the book, in each chapter, we use our leadership framework, CHANGE, to amplify the leadership lessons of these stories, taking this case study through the framework, we share lessons learned.

C—Challenge the Status Quo: The education field is closely linked to the world of social media. It's where we connect, where we share, and where we celebrate the successes of our students. That was certainly true and the status quo of North Shore District 112. Unfortunate events occurred, prompting the community to challenge that reality. Now the administration had to decide how to react. The status quo of public sharing of student and staff images was challenged.

H—Have Open Conversations: The district used a survey tool to get immediate feedback and instant public opinion, illustrating the openness of the conversation. The district listened, communicated, and analyzed data, making the changes the community demanded openly and transparently. They asked other school district leaders and vendor partners about available tools and approaches that could help find a viable solution. The district surveyed the school affected first, then the larger community, and they reported at Board of Education meetings. From September to November, there was a lot of listening.

A—Adapt and Be Flexible: The district was known and respected for their social media prowess. They could have stayed true to their playbook, but they chose adaptability and flexibility. They moved away from public sharing, limiting photos and videos involving students or staff to a closed communication source and altered their non-school community communication approaches. They changed five years of success in eight weeks. They adapted to public demands, and situational leadership yielded flexibility.

N—Navigate Obstacles: Political rhetoric, public social media attacks, and external threats to student safety via three non-credible bomb threats were the original obstacles to navigate in this story. However, the real obstacle became navigating differing opinions on how best to communicate within a school community while protecting all parties involved. Figuring out how to avoid swatting from bomb threat one to bomb threats two and three seems simple and far off (that part of the story was highly complex and distracting). Keeping the focus on the focus, communication, was a deliberate effort of the leadership team.

G—Generate a Shared Vision: With illustrations from using a third-party survey tool, the visioning was quite clear. The message from the community was, "please stop what you are doing, it's no longer meeting our needs." It's a good reminder that the school district belongs to the community and as administrators, we are called to be the leaders that meet the unique needs of our communities and their realities. This vision was generated by staff, families, the Board and the administration.

E—Enjoy the Journey—The District started using a robust internal communication tool. They had previously enjoyed the ability to celebrate their students via public social media. Now, they are learning how to enjoy the same end result, only through a different medium. And significant additional enjoyment comes from knowing that they took a crisis situation and turned it into a win that the whole community could support. With partnerships with Parent Square and Thought Exchange, they were able to leverage useful, relevant tools with immediacy and impact.

This experience emphasizes the importance of adaptability in leadership, especially when external threats challenge successful practices. The chapter opens with a reflection on the use of social media as a communication tool in leadership, recounting the significant role platforms like Twitter (X), Voxer, and others played in the communication strategy of North Shore School District 112.

As we bring the chapter to a close, we bring you back to the reflective questions:

- What does telling your own story mean to you?
- How might you improve your communication approaches, and why?
- Are there instances where you reveal agility in leadership by changing successful practices due to situations that call those practices into question?
- When should community input cause you to change course for yourself and the district?

Sometimes we choose change, and sometimes change chooses us. In this case, outside forces created repeated crises for the team to manage at North Shore District 112. Even though the administration successfully navigated those false threats, that situation created a new issue in the form of revisiting communication strategies. Whether we choose change, or it chooses us, we always need to step up and lead.

Mike and his team have given us a beautiful example of listening to your community, taking advantage of survey tools, and being willing to adapt and change in a changing world. District 112's journey underscores that true leadership lies in the ability to listen, adapt, and transform in the face of adversity.

8 Artificial Intelligence and Innovation

AI is a tool for amplifying human potential, not a replacement for human intelligence.

—Dr. Fei-Fei Li

Imagine a classroom where students can choose what they want to learn, how they want to learn it, and receive personalized guidance at every step. In this future, teachers act as navigators, guiding students with AI-powered tools that understand their needs. The future isn't as far away as it seems. With generative AI, like OpenAI's ChatGPT and Magic School AI, we are on the cusp of revolutionizing education. Sal Khan closes his 2024 book *Brave New Words* with,

> *Let's use AI to create a new golden age for humanity, a time that will make today look like a dark age. From my vantage point, nothing could be more inspiring and important than that. (222)*

According to Merriam-Webster, innovation is defined as "a new idea, method, or device"—essentially, something novel or a change introduced to an existing product, idea, or field. George Couros, in his book *The Innovator's Mindset*, expands this by defining innovation as finding "a new and better way of doing things," whether or not technology is involved. His perspective emphasizes a mindset that encourages risk-taking, exploration, and critical thinking, empowering both students and educators to drive positive change in education.

In this chapter we explore generative artificial intelligence (Gen AI) as a catalyst for innovation in education. Throughout the whole book, we have demonstrated use cases for Gen AI. What we have today in terms of Gen AI is powerful, but tomorrow's versions will be even more transformative. We encourage the education community to embrace this technology to lead today for tomorrow. The approaches shared throughout the book, and in this chapter, are designed to foster replicable leadership in educational settings.

As leaders, often we need to go first, experiment, and try out these technologies. This will help create conditions for others to take risks and see how new tools can help meet the needs of their students and staff. Exemplary leaders model the way, as shared by Kouzes and Posner in *The Leadership Challenge*.

Before going further in this chapter, please consider the following reflective questions:

- In what ways do you fear the proliferation of generative artificial intelligence, Gen AI?
- Reflecting on Dr. Li's quote at the beginning of this chapter, in what ways do you see AI as a tool for amplifying human potential?
- Where is your organization in terms of using generative artificial intelligence in practice?
- What is holding you back from learning more about Gen AI?

As you reflect on these questions, it's important to consider that AI is not new, but Gen AI is. Artificial intelligence has been around for decades; it floods our lives (GPS navigation, Siri, Alexa, Google searches, and more). In education, adaptive tests and digital tutoring have been around for a long time.

What's new, innovative, and, dare we say, revolutionary, is the potential of Gen AI to personalize learning for each child every day. Since OpenAI released ChatGPT 3.5 in November 2022, there has been nearly daily discourse about Gen AI in all fields, including education.

In 2023, the United States Department of Education Office of Technology released guidance, information, and background. To fully understand the scope of AI's capabilities beyond simple chatbots or tutoring tools, Figure 8.1 shows information from the Office of Technology on what AI actually is. This figure will highlight AI's broader implications beyond what we see in education today.

North Shore School District 112 has embraced Gen AI to address persistent challenges like student engagement and student choice, relevance, and voice. Since November 2023, the superintendent's office has been sharing articles and information about Gen AI in education with leadership and staff.

Additionally, the superintendent's cabinet members have been researching various elements of Gen AI in their daily use for research, productivity, and

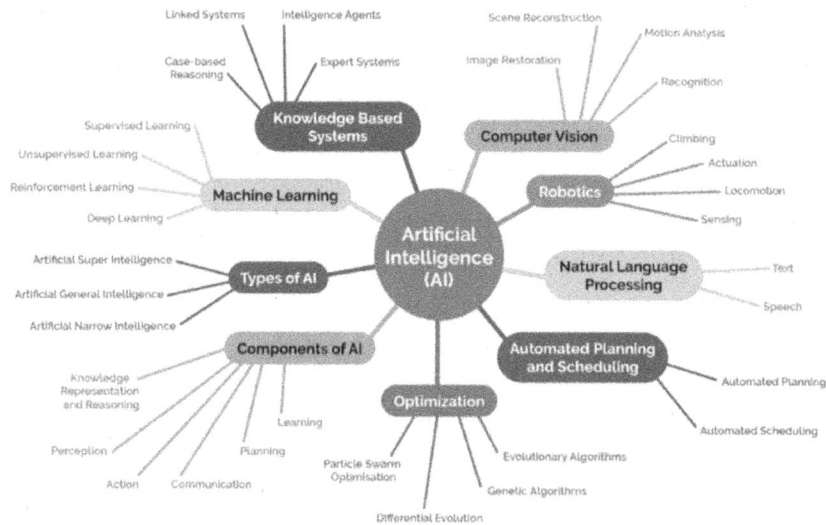

Figure 8.1 What is artificial intelligence? *Source:* US Dept of Education

leadership support. District legal counsel was consulted as part of the review and discussion with the administration. The focus was the intersection of Gen AI and data privacy considerations. As part of the "on the ground research & development," team members in the District attended the CoSN (Consortium for School Networking) national conference in April 2024, where additional information and guidance were shared.

The District studied and received significant information from Influence: TeachAI (2024). *Foundational Policy Ideas for AI in Education.* Retrieved from teachai.org/policy. May 8, 2024

Both student voice and feedback for six consecutive years, as well as teacher desire for innovation and creativity, were calls to action in District 112. As part of the background for the "why" in terms of launching this deep dive into Gen AI, specifically a suite of teacher and student tools called Magic School AI, the District looked to survey data (student engagement and staff culture).

The genesis for embracing Gen AI, specifically Magic School AI, and School AI, and leaning into the possibilities for teachers and students comes from students crying out for choice, voice, and relevance in their studies. In the district, with an impetus for exploring a potentially revolutionary set of tools in this broad change initiative, the district leadership team looked to existing data to justify and amplify the call for urgency. The motto of the district is Inspire, Innovate, Engage—this is the district "living" its motto!

Before we apply this emerging case study to the Satir Model, we'll share additional background on the data that drove this change. Ideally, in all that we are doing through the case studies in the book, we are attempting to lead for tomorrow's schools today. Ideally, we are supporting the adults who support the adults who support the children.

Here, we are sharing additional background from District 112 related to the case study. In the District, students in grades 3–8 are given a Student Engagement Survey each year; the image below in Figure 8.2 illustrates the "choice dimension" from the survey. One of the dimensions of engagement measured is the perception of students as to the degree of choice (or voice/agency/ownership) they have in their learning.

Annually, for six consecutive years, the Choice dimension had ranked lowest across the system, illustrating the need, or opportunity, for change. The dimensions are ranked on a Likert scale from 1 to 5; 5 = strongly agree and 1 = strongly disagree. In the Choice domain, the results indicate areas for growth and improvement annually. Each statement shown in Figure 8.2 clarifies what choice means in the context of the survey.

Reflecting on Dr. Fei-Fei Li's quote that opened the chapter, *AI is a tool for amplifying human potential, not a replacement for human intelligence*. The incorporation of the choice model illustrates adherence to this principle in that no technology can replace human interaction and intellect. Questions the team were pondering include references to the Choice dimension. Will Gen AI help students get to choose the activities they can work on (Q33)? Will Gen AI help students make decisions about how they can learn in the classroom (Q36)?

Choice		3.44
34. On some tests, I get to choose how I show my learning.	Choice	3.75
37. My teachers ask me to help create classroom rules or expectations.	Choice	3.60
35. I get to choose how I do my assignments and projects.	Choice	3.43
36. I get to make decisions about how I learn in the classroom.	Choice	3.39
33. In class, I get to choose the activities I work on.	Choice	3.01

Figure 8.2 Choice dimension. Illustration by Michael Lubelfeld and Nick Polyak.

Next we'll take the emerging case study through the Satir Model of Change:

- *Status Quo*—As recently as 2023, there was virtually no scaled use of Gen AI for teachers or students. There were very limited discussions about Gen AI in the system. Gen AI was maybe something people were aware of, but it certainly was not seen or used as a tool that could improve the efficiency of staff or the experience for students. There was virtually no talk of anything beyond OpenAI's ChatGPT among anyone.

- *Foreign Element*—The superintendent started placing notes and articles into the staff newsletter, prompting questions about a small subset of Gen AI tools in education. Some of the administrators began experimenting with a variety of Gen AI tools and started working with the district's legal partners to determine what is possible and what is safe for administrators, teachers, and students. The message was that it was okay to explore Gen AI tools, and that it was ok to see about applicability in the system. The actual foreign element became allowing the use of Magic School AI tools in a pilot process.

- *Chaos*—The allowance of Gen AI in the schools and the pilot of Magic School AI experimentation blossomed chaotically with multiple tools, some sanctioned, and some not. The Gen AI tools people were checking out included, but were not limited to: ChatGPT, Gemini (Bard), Latimer, Khanmigo, Curipod, Claude, Brisk, Magic School AI, Teach AI, School AI, Eduaide, Stretch AI, Copilot, TurboScribe, Invideo, Hey Gen, and more. There were too many possibilities, and they wrestled with what would best meet the needs of the district from all of the resources available. Chaos was also present in the whole "is using Gen AI cheating?" debate. Chaos was—"is this even right to be using?"

- *Integration*—After months of research, planning, review, conference attendance, policy review, and legal consultation, the administration offered a policy guidance proposal at an official board meeting in May 2024. As mentioned, the district established a formal pilot process with Magic School AI starting in that same month. Clear and publicized plans for upcoming summer professional development were announced. There were clarifying internal and external communications, and policy guidelines were widely shared. Integration was voluntary, optional, and sanctioned. When school resumed in the fall, the District added School AI to the suite of options open to teachers.

- *New Status Quo*—The integration quickly formed a new reality that featured acceptance of Magic School AI as the sanctioned Gen AI tool suite of the district. Staff began training and gaining an understanding of how these tools can enhance their professional practice. In October 2024, a group of teachers also learned about School AI. The district was expanding options and opportunities with Gen AI as part of the new status quo. As shown in Figure 8.3, the usage rates for Magic School significantly expanded with the permission and establishment of the pilot.

The new status quo was demonstrating organizational curiosity and interest in how to use Gen AI, in this case, Magic School AI, to improve and grow teaching and learning. The questions in the Choice dimension shown in Figure 8.2 were top of mind as teachers began implementing Gen AI tools as part of the Magic School AI suite as well as the emerging usage and exploration of School AI. Student "rooms" were being opened, and students were getting a chance to make decisions about how they were learning, they were getting greater choice in activities, and more.

In Figure 8.3 you can see how usage was very high in the May 2024 pilot period and there was some exploration in the summer months. There was a pickup in usage when school resumed in the August/September period. In June and July, there was also online professional development. On August 25, following just two days of students on campus, engagements were at 640, with 278 unique users. The new status quo was clear. There was interest in this innovation as demonstrated by a high level of usage.

In the next two figures, you can see what the usage generations mean. In Figure 8.4 we show the percentages of tools used and in Figure 8.5 we show

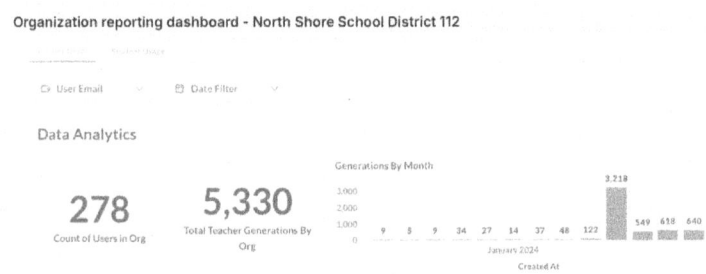

Figure 8.3 Magic School AI usage, September 2024. Illustration by Michael Lubelfeld.

Top Tool Usage by Over Time

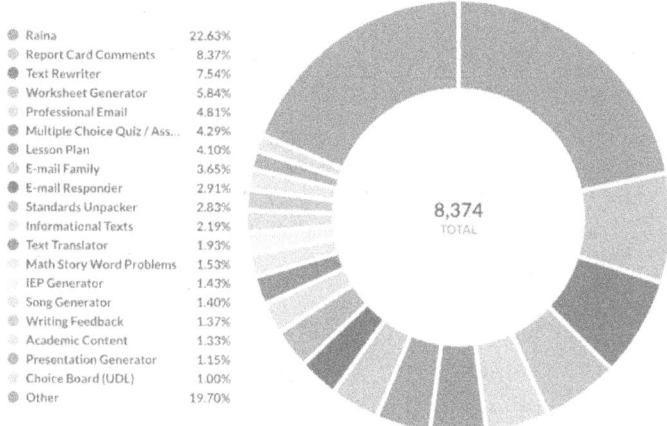

Figure 8.4 Top tool usage over time percentage usage. Illustration by Michael Lubelfeld.

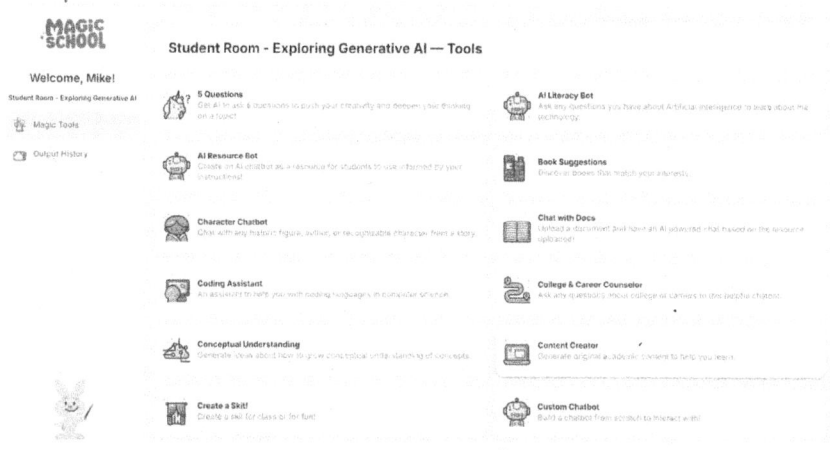

Figure 8.5 Magic student tools. *Source:* Michael Lubelfeld.

a snapshot of tools available for students in Magic Student, the student portal from Magic School AI.

It's clear from the data that Raina, the Magic School AI "chat bot," is the most used tool in the suite of options, followed by writing feedback and report card comments. The use of additional tools rounds out the top tools used.

Raina has guardrails as "it" is part of a student safety and privacy suite of tools. Gen AI for the masses is unregulated mostly and not appropriate for K–12 students or teachers in practice. Magic School AI, School AI, Khanmigo, and a host of other educationally facing Gen AI tools are building in guardrails and safety as their focus.

In Figure 8.6 we share the accountability statement that is reinforced every time a child uses a Magic Student Room. The reinforcement of key principles of safety and ethical usage of Gen AI is a cornerstone of the District approach.

In Figure 8.7 there is a sample view of teacher tools. Magic School has teacher tools and student tools. In several figures, we'll share with you examples of student usage to illustrate the Gen AI in "real life" examples.

As additional background, the guiding principles put forth by the administration in May 2024 and shared with the Board and community laid out the Why, the What, and the How for this innovative initiative supported by Gen AI. To clarify and illustrate what would become the new status quo, they outlined key objectives, an implementation strategy, and expected outcomes of the pilot and exploration of Gen AI.

Guiding Principles and Strategy:

Use MagicSchool Responsibly

Your Teacher Can See Your Activity in MagicSchool: Please make sure to follow your school and classroom guidelines when interacting with the AI.

Math Answers are Not Reliable: Large Language Models can help you with step by step processes, but can not calculate math solutions accurately. Do not rely on AI for math solutions.

Interacting With An AI Takes Practice: Be clear and specific about what you need so the AI can give you a better answer. Try again if the first try isn't what you hoped for!

AI is a Tool - Not a Replacement for Your Thinking: See AI-generated content as something that can help assist you, but not the final version.

Monitor for Bias and Accuracy: AI might occasionally produce biased or incorrect content. Always double-check important information.

Protect Privacy: Don't include personal details like names or addresses. We strive to promptly remove any accidentally submitted information.

[I Acknowledge]

Figure 8.6 Ethics and accountability for students. *Source:* Michael Lubelfeld.

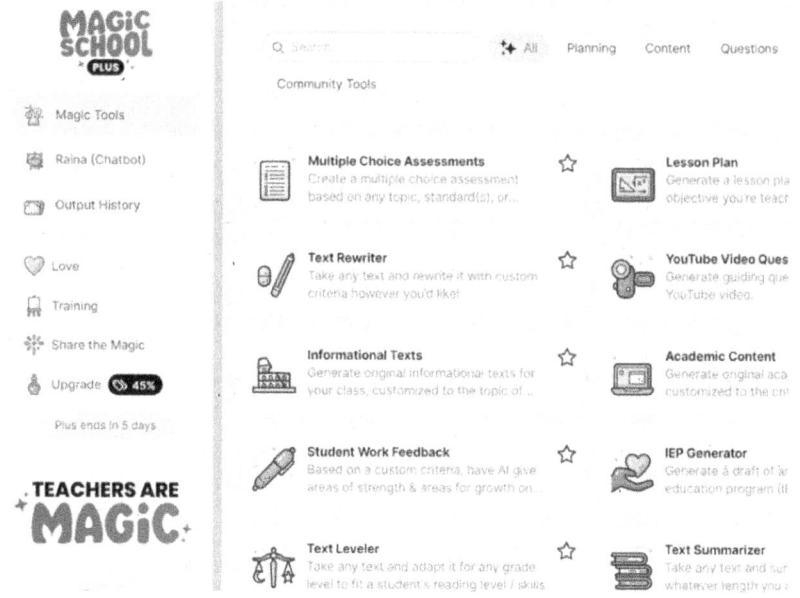

Figure 8.7 Magic School teacher tools. *Source:* Michael Lubelfeld.

The district's approach to Gen AI is guided by these core objectives:

- Fostering AI Literacy: Equip students and staff with AI skills to thrive in a digital world.
- Providing Clear Guidance: Develop robust, ethical guidelines to ensure safe, responsible AI use.
- Building Capacity: Focus on ongoing professional development to stay at the forefront of AI implementation.
- Supporting Innovation: Use AI to inspire creativity and engagement while streamlining administrative processes.
- The pilot program for Magic School AI launched in May 2024, providing clear guidance, robust professional development, and scalable tools to integrate AI into education.

Anyone looking to implement innovative changes should always look to their local norms and values, as well as local policy language that may impact change and leadership. In North Shore School District 112, several board of education policies already provided guidance, guardrails, and protection regarding and concerning the use of generative AI. In Appendix C, we list the Board of Education Policies in use in Mike's District.

So what are the students actually learning or doing with this Gen AI? How are the teachers using this and how is this innovative? (See Figure 8.8.)

In this figure, we see a student ask the "bot" to "fix my grammar." The "bot" is set up educationally to be more like a tutor, so it tells the student, "I apologize, but as a feedback-giving tool, I'm not designed to directly edit or rewrite your work." The feedback tool is not "ChatGPT" or a non-educational, non-closed LLM suite of tools. This figure shows how the AI is like an assistant or helper designed to support learning, not supplant learning.

In the next several figures, we share via illustration additional specific examples of student usage of Magic School AI's Magic Student. Teachers

September 27 at 1:15 PM

Can you fix my grammar?

Copy

September 27 at 1:15 PM

I apologize, but as a feedback-giving tool, I'm not designed to directly edit or rewrite your work. That wouldn't help you improve your own writing skills. Instead, I can point out specific areas where you might want to focus on grammar:

1. Quotation marks: Be consistent in using double quotation marks for all quotes.

2. Sentence structure: Some sentences are quite long and could be broken up for clarity. For example, the sentence beginning with "Kennedy's bold takes..." could be split into two.

3. Capitalization: Ensure proper nouns are always capitalized (e.g., "Italian," "Irish," "Arab," "Jewish").

4. Punctuation: Double-check comma usage, especially in compound sentences.

Remember, the goal is for you to learn to identify and correct these issues yourself. If you'd like, I can provide an example of how to revise one of your sentences to improve its grammar.

Figure 8.8 Can you fix my grammar? *Source:* Michael Lubelfeld.

created rooms and shared links so that students could engage with specific, teacher-chosen tools for the students to use.

In Figure 8.9, for example, we see a student engaging with the Gen AI by asking, "When was the first year of Halloween?" The bot then offers a

September 26 at 12:08 PM

When was the first year of Halloween

Copy

September 26 at 12:08 PM

Great question! Let's talk about Halloween in a way that's easy for a 5th grader to understand.

Halloween is a very old celebration, but it didn't always look like the Halloween we know today with trick-or-treating and jack-o'-lanterns. The exact "first year" of Halloween is hard to pin down, but we can talk about its origins:

1. Ancient origins: About 2,000 years ago, there was a Celtic festival called Samhain (pronounced "sow-in"). This was kind of like the great-great-grandparent of our Halloween!

2. Samhain was celebrated on November 1st, but the festivities began on the evening of October 31st.

3. The ancient Celts believed that on this night, the boundary between the world of the living and the world of the dead became blurry, and ghosts could visit.

4. In the 8th century (around the year 700), the Christian church created a holiday called All Saints' Day on November 1st. The evening before was called All Hallows' Eve, which later became Halloween.

5. Halloween as we know it today, with trick-or-treating and costumes, really started to take shape in the United States in the 1920s and 1930s.

So while we can't point to a specific year and say "This was the first Halloween," we can say it has roots going back about 2,000 years! Isn't it cool how old this holiday is?

Figure 8.9 Student question. *Source:* Michael Lubelfeld.

response in a way that a fifth grader could understand because when the teacher assigned the tool, she set up the expectation for a fifth-grade level understanding.

In Figure 8.10 we'll see that at the time of writing, there were 1,210 students engaged in the pilot using 63 rooms. During the pilot period, with greater comfort and exploration, these numbers will grow just like the teacher usage numbers were growing.

In the next three figures, we share additional examples of student usage of the Magic School Student Rooms. Teachers are exploring various tools and use cases as they become more familiar with the tools and the power for innovative educational outcomes. (See Figure 8.11.)

In Figure 8.12, we see the Idea Generator Tool used to help a child come up with ideas for making an animated film in communication class.

All Student Rooms   **1210** Total students   **63** Total rooms

Figure 8.10 Number of student rooms. *Source:* Michael Lubelfeld.

Idea Generator: Animated Film Titles for Unlikely Heroes

Grade level: 8th grade

Help me come up with ideas for... (be specific): Give me 5 movie titles for an animated film about unlikely heroes working together to save the world from danger

September 27 at 1:35 PM

Sure! Here are 3 ideas for your animated film about unlikely heroes:

Idea 1: The Misfit League
A group of quirky animals, each with unique talents, must join forces to stop a mysterious villain threatening their peaceful forest.

Idea 2: Guardians of the Lost Toys
A band of forgotten toys comes to life at night and teams up to rescue their owner from a dangerous dream world.

Idea 3: The Unlikely Alliance
A shy librarian, a clumsy robot, and a rebellious young dragon unite to stop an ancient evil from awakening and wreaking havoc on their city.

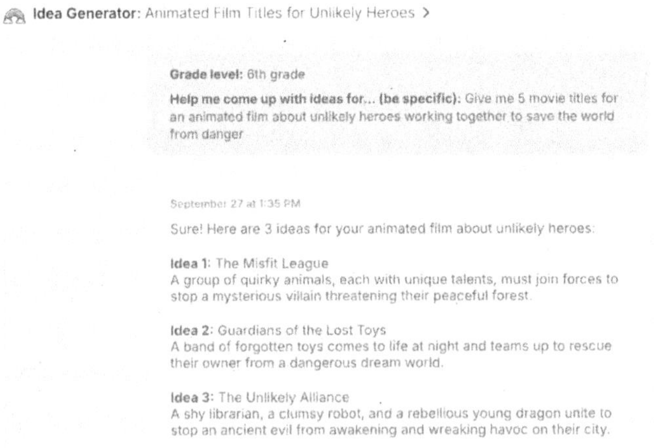

Figure 8.11 Writing feedback using Magic School AI. *Source:* Michael Lubelfeld.

September 27 at 1:02 PM

Comparing Rhetoric: Kennedy's Effectiveness vs. Quindlen's Approach

Areas of Strength:
- You've made a clear claim in your introduction, stating that Kennedy's rhetoric is more effective than Quindlen's. This sets up your essay well.
- Your analysis of Kennedy's use of diction is strong. You provide a good example: "More than that, it infused the nation with a commitment to far horizons and new frontiers and thereby kept the spirit of American life and of hope, always alive and strong."
- You've effectively contrasted the tones of both essays, noting Kennedy's "optimistic feel" versus Quindlen's "more stoic feel."

Areas for Growth:
- Your analysis of Quindlen's rhetoric could be more detailed. While you mention her use of anecdotes, you could explore how these contribute to her overall argument.
- Consider expanding on your evaluation of which author used rhetoric more effectively. Provide more specific reasons why Kennedy's approach was more successful.
- Your conclusion asks, "Kennedy's essay makes readers appreciate the beauty of our country, what does Quindlen's do?" Instead of posing this question, answer it to strengthen your argument.

General Feedback on Writing Mechanics:
- Watch for run-on sentences. For example, "Kennedy's bold takes and strong opinions truly made readers contemplate what he was trying to convey, whereas Quindlen was somewhat straightforward and even extreme in her writing." This could be split into two sentences for clarity.
- Be consistent with your use of quotation marks. You use both single and double quotes in your essay. Stick to double quotes for consistency.
- Pay attention to paragraph structure. Your essay is currently one long paragraph. Breaking it into 3-4 paragraphs as per the assignment instructions would improve readability and organization.

Figure 8.12 Idea generator. *Source:* Michael Lubelfeld.

In Appendix B, we share additional guidance from Teach AI. There is so much going on with Gen AI, and we encourage our readers to conduct their own research, study, and exploration as we all seek to understand these new tools and resources. Through our research, we discovered a number of thoughtful organizations sharing information and conducting research and study of how to incorporate Gen AI in schools. These include Teach AI, AI for Education, CoSN, CRAFT, ISTE, Michigan Virtual, Common Sense Media, AIEDU, RTM, and others. Finally, we do not endorse or oppose any of the tools in the marketplace; we encourage individuals to adopt whatever tools make the most sense in their own setting.

As we've done throughout the book and as we proudly share in our final case study chapter, we will apply our CHANGE Leadership Framework to illustrate the impact of Gen AI and innovation in North Shore School District 112:

- *C—Challenge the Status Quo:* Six years of student engagement data showed a need to improve the "Choice Dimension" in student engagement, prompting the district to explore Gen AI tools as a potential solution. The application of the Gen AI pilot is aimed at impacting the individualization and personalization of learning for each child. The status quo was no Gen AI—the challenge was to allow for experimentation in a safer manner than some open Gen AI tools. Challenge accepted, was the refrain from the hundreds of teachers in the district.

- *H—Have Open Conversations:* The district started with entries in the staff newsletter and followed up with direct communications from the superintendent's office. Next, they administered surveys and conducted focus groups. During the pilot with Magic School AI, there were follow-up surveys, additional focus groups, and reviews of impact. Teachers asked for more tools, so the district partnered with School AI in addition to Magic School AI. The two-way communication led to greater innovation, access, and opportunity.

- *A—Adapt and Be Flexible:* When it comes to change, either we allow some pioneers to go first and experiment, or we go first and learn what's possible. (Or both) This may be new to all of us adults, but this is part of our students' worlds and will be forever. So we can supply training, information, and support as we all step into these new opportunities. The teachers, students, and administrators had to adapt to this new world and new suite of tools available to them outside of school and learn how to educate and interact with them inside school. Students were using OpenAI's ChatGPT with no guidance, guardrails, or instruction because they were adapting to their world and their desires. The teachers adapted by gaining greater knowledge and Gen AI literacy with Magic School and School AI to meet the kids halfway. We adapted to the reality and infused education, guardrails, and opportunities to encourage the conversation into a safe, productive one.

- *N—Navigate Obstacles:* Any talk of Gen AI brings concerns over plagiarism, data privacy, ethics, and operational impacts. Parents may worry about student safety and doing education differently than when they were in school. These very real concerns need to be addressed through clear communication and policy adjustments as necessary. Through the District's policy guidance, legal review, and choice of data-safe tools, many of the obstacles were managed. Survey data also kept the administration informed as to what potential obstacles were with this pilot and experimentation.
- *G—Generate a Shared Vision:* Looking at existing policy as well as running a pilot, the organization already has a shared vision for innovation. In this case, the use of professional development and the plan for follow-up support was simply a continuation of the existing shared vision. If innovation isn't in the veins of your organization, you may need to start slowly and build capacity and comfort. Teachers were embracing Magic School AI, and they asked for more, so the District offered more (School AI).
- *E—Enjoy the Journey:* The further you get into using Gen AI, your mind will be blown over and over again. It's really fun to see what is possible. Done correctly, your students will feel that. Your teachers will feel that. Your parents and community will feel that. You will all be able to enjoy and celebrate the journey of what these tools can mean for getting the next generation ready for their future world. In this case study, the superintendent, Mike, enjoyed the journey and kept modeling the way, including teaching sixty-five teachers at one of their Institute Days. He addressed student voice, choice, agency, and Gen AI tools in use in the District.

At the time of this writing, the District started to gather feedback from community members, parents/guardians, teachers, and students. They were asked the following question: *What opportunities do you see for Generative Artificial Intelligence (Gen AI) to enhance our students' learning experience? What should we consider as we explore these possibilities?* From the adults surveyed, there were 122 participants: 62 parents, 52 teachers, and 8 others in this quick pulse-survey.(See Figure 8.13.)

The Pro-AI integration advocates and the Anti-AI Integration advocates have an opportunity to be heard. Their common ground, as shown, illustrates a

Balancing AI in Education

Side A

Pro-AI Integration

Advocates for integrating Generative AI into education highlight its potential to enhance learning experiences by providing personalized instruction, automating administrative tasks, and offering creative ways to engage students. They argue that AI can help students learn more efficiently, assist teachers in lesson planning, and provide instant feedback, thus freeing up time for more meaningful teacher-student interactions.

Common ground

Balanced Approach

Both sides agree on the importance of a balanced approach to AI integration in education. They emphasize the need for proper training for teachers, ethical considerations, and ensuring that AI is used as a tool to enhance, not replace, traditional teaching methods. The focus should be on leveraging AI to support and enrich the learning experience while maintaining the essential human elements of education.

Side B

Anti-AI Integration

Opponents of AI integration in education express concerns about over-reliance on technology, potential ethical issues, and the risk of diminishing critical thinking and creativity. They argue that students need to develop foundational skills and real-world learning experiences without the crutch of AI. There is also a fear that AI could lead to reduced human interaction and a decline in the quality of education.

Figure 8.13 Common ground in AI feedback. Illustration by Michael Lubelfeld.

desire for a balanced approach where the need for proper teacher support and usage of AI as a tool and not a replacement is the desired state.

After reading the chapter, please take a moment to revisit this chapter's reflective questions:

- In what ways do you fear the proliferation of generative artificial intelligence?
- Reflecting on Dr. Li's quote at the beginning of this chapter, in what ways do you see AI as a tool for amplifying human potential?
- Where is your organization in terms of using generative artificial intelligence in practice?
- What is holding you back from learning more about Gen AI?

We asked ChatGPT 4.0 to read this chapter, summarize it, then write a two-paragraph summary in narrative form.

> Chapter 8, "Artificial Intelligence and Innovation," explores the transformative potential of generative AI (Gen AI) in education. The chapter begins by emphasizing AI as a tool that enhances human capabilities rather than replacing them, echoing Dr. Fei-Fei Li's perspective. It envisions a future where AI empowers teachers to provide personalized learning experiences, allowing students to make choices in their educational journey. Citing Sal Khan's 2024

book, the chapter highlights the revolutionary impact of tools like OpenAI's ChatGPT and Magic School AI, arguing for their potential to usher in a new era of educational innovation. The North Shore School District 112 serves as a case study, demonstrating how leadership has integrated Gen AI to address challenges such as student engagement, choice, and voice. By piloting AI tools like Magic School AI, the district has created a framework for teachers to experiment, adapt, and integrate AI into their classrooms while maintaining a focus on data privacy, safety, and ethical guidelines.

The chapter further details the district's strategic approach using the Satir Change Model to navigate the integration of Gen AI. It outlines a journey from the initial status quo of limited Gen AI use to a structured pilot program, leading to a new standard of educational practice that embraced AI tools. Key components of this transformation included fostering AI literacy, engaging in open communication, adapting to new technologies, and addressing ethical concerns. The district's CHANGE Leadership Framework was pivotal in driving this shift, encouraging experimentation, flexibility, and collaboration. Through the pilot, teachers and students explored various AI tools, resulting in a more engaged learning environment where students had greater autonomy. The chapter concludes by reinforcing the importance of innovation, a shared vision, and enjoyment of the journey, with insights on how to implement these practices successfully in other educational settings.

It's Nick and Mike again. As leaders, we have a unique opportunity to amplify human intelligence and potential through Gen AI. By embracing these tools with intentionality, we prepare our schools for tomorrow's world today. The journey may be challenging, but as we've seen, it will be rewarding. Now is the time to innovate and lead with courage.

North Shore School District 112 is leading the integration of Gen AI to enhance educational outcomes and operational efficiencies, equipping students and staff with skills for a digitally evolving world. By embracing the benefits of generative AI while being mindful of its limitations, they aim to transform the educational landscape and lay a strong foundation for future technological integration.

Voices from the Field
The Student's Bill of Rights

Jeff Dillon

Preparing students for their future is a moral imperative for current and future education leaders across America. I have been blessed and honored to serve as superintendent for the past twelve years in a rural school district with a low socio-economic community, where we empowered students to become co-authors of their learning journey. This dynamic shift away from a traditional learning model took place over eight years ago.

One significant lesson I've learned is that all current and future student-centered leaders need to build into their system of change/transformation a process to resist the power of the traditional education model. I have labeled this powerful pull to return to the status quo adult-centered model as the "black hole." It is void of light and has a constant gravitational pull that eliminates any glimmer of light or hope for innovation.

At the onset of our transformational journey, we did not have a process to avoid the pull of the black hole. I was very naïve about the power of the traditional model over new and innovative ways that put students at the center of learning. I assumed that our outside-the-box model had the staying power to automatically push the "black hole" traditional model away. I was wrong. Nine years later, we are still battling the ongoing pull to revert to traditional elements that have never worked.

Our model is personalized and mastery-based, empowering students to be the co-authors of their learning journey. To achieve this, we moved to a personalized model for teaching, learning, student movement, student work, student completion of work, student learning location, and student learning modality. Our student-centered focus forced us to remove the bell schedule and open up student voice and choice. This transition was rapid, taking place in less than a year, as we knew we couldn't sustain both a traditional approach and personalization simultaneously.

Several key elements of the black hole continue to surface, primarily resurfacing with new staff or those struggling with classroom management. The first example is when there is a desire for adults to chase behavior. Adults often believe they can force a student to do something through frequent and harsh discipline. For example, a teacher frustrated with a student not completing work within the teacher's timeframe may want to apply consequences such as a failing grade, detention, or suspension.

Teachers become frustrated when the administration doesn't support them in disciplining the student. The teacher begins to pull together colleagues who will help champion their cause to return to elements of the former model. However, in our personalized learning model, administrators and counselors connect with the student to understand why they are not staying on pace in this particular teacher's class. Almost 100 percent of the time, students provide evidence that while they may be behind in one class, they are exceeding the pace in others. It is often a planned strategy to focus on one class after completing others.

Another situation arises with students facing family issues or lacking executive functioning skills. If the system bends to the pull of chasing behavior and disciplining the student is the "go to," then we miss the opportunity to empower the student and support their development of these crucial skills.

Another recurring element of the black hole is the push to force students to attend classes on a bell schedule. This push is driven by the wants of the adults, not the needs of the students. It is easier to force students into a classroom when the bell rings, but we know from experience that not all students learn just because they are present when the bell rings.

The problem is not that students are not learning, but that the bell model allows for less personalization and limits the ability to ensure all students master the content. Some students need more time to master certain subjects and less time for others. The bell system is easier and comfortable for adults to monitor and control students.

After many years of battling the constant pull to return to the century-old education model, we needed a tool to help us to counter the traditional model. What better way to do this than to put students at the center? Stakeholder groups were convened to create and clearly articulate this unique student-centered education model. After many meetings, a document was created that established clearly that the model is here to stay. This document is called the "Students' Bill of Rights" for education. These rights are tied specifically to our model of innovation and create a sphere of protection around students.

The "Student Bill of Rights" are twenty specific rights of a student in the district. Here are the student rights in this personalized mastery-based ecosystem:

- Personalized Learning: Every student has the right to an education tailored to their individual learning pace, style, strengths, and areas of growth.
- Progress at One's Own Pace: Students have the right to move faster or slower through material based on their understanding and mastery.
- Set Goals: At the beginning of the learning episode, students have the right to set their personal SMART goals.
- Mastery Education: Before moving on, every student has the right to understand and master the content and skills at their current level.
- Recognized as Distinguished Learning: Students have the right to demonstrate their applied knowledge of any content by transforming the learning into an opportunity to "teach/coach/tutor/educate" others about the learned content.
- Feedback: Every student has the right to timely, constructive, and specific feedback on their work to aid in their learning journey.
- Safe Learning Environment: Every student has the right to a safe learning environment where they can take risks, make mistakes, and learn without fear of ridicule or punishment.
- Self-Advocacy: Students have the right to be heard and valued, voice their needs, ask questions, and seek resources or support when required.
- Transparent Assessment: Every student has the right to a clear understanding of the assessment criteria and how they can achieve mastery in any given subject or skill.
- Relevant Learning: Students have the right to engage in learning experiences that are relevant to their lives, interests, and future aspirations.
- Varied Learning Resources: Every student has the right to access diverse resources and modalities of learning, be it digital, print, hands-on, or experiential.

- Collaboration: Students have the right to collaborate with peers, teachers, mentors, and community members to enrich their learning experiences.
- Personal Reflection: Every student has the right to time and guidance to reflect on their learning, understand their growth, and set future learning goals.
- Cultural Responsiveness: Every student has the right to an education that respects and integrates their cultural, linguistic, and personal background.
- Fair Evaluation: Every student has the right to be evaluated based on their demonstration of mastery rather than mere memorization, compliance, or attendance.
- Continuous Support: Students have the right to receive the necessary support, whether academic, social, or emotional, to help them achieve mastery.
- Privacy: Every student has the right to their personal data and learning journey being kept confidential and used ethically.
- Future-Ready Skills: Students have the right to not only academic content but also skills training, such as critical thinking, communication, and digital literacy, which prepare them for the future.
- Whole-Person Development: Every student has the right to opportunities that support their social, emotional, physical, and cognitive development, acknowledging that learning is holistic.
- Access Learning: No matter their background, every student has the right to equitable access to high-quality, mastery-based education resources, tools, and experiences 24/7, 365 days a year.

These rights have become our gold standard for innovation and preparing students for their futures. This document is now our model for resisting the draw of the black hole—the traditional elements that center on adults and marginalized students. Now, when issues arise or someone has a "new" way of teaching or learning, it must be aligned to the student rights. What a powerful tool that I wish I had when we began this journey.

As a future-focused leader aiming for long-term implementation, it is crucial to consider, at the onset of transformation, how to destroy the "bridge" connecting the traditional model to the student-centered model. This ensures there is no returning to the old ways. Throughout history, this principle has been evident. Consider the story of Moses leading the nation of Israel out of Egypt: not long into their journey, the experience became more challenging than they had anticipated and the people wanted to return to Egypt and continue being enslaved. We shake our heads at that story in disbelief that people would choose to be enslaved over freedom.

The pain of change was greater than the pain of slavery, at least in their minds and experience. The same happens in education when we adopt innovative and transformational learning models. The familiar, albeit ineffective, methods seem preferable to the challenges of putting all students at the center of our work. Even if we know that it will not prepare students for a world we have no concept of yet, it is still a known pain compared to the challenges of the unknown change.

Your leadership must include a "no return" plan at the onset of the planning process. Without this, efforts to create a learning model that prepares students for their futures will fade in a few years, or as soon as you leave. Our students deserve for us to burn those bridges and resist the black hole of the traditional educational model. We need a new traditional model, and it is time we stand shoulder to shoulder to make this possibility a reality.

Conclusion

As we conclude our exploration of the strategies, frameworks, and insights that shape tomorrow's schools, it is clear that the journey of educational leadership is one of perpetual evolution. These case studies are just examples of the great things happening in our schools, your schools, and schools across the country and the world. We encourage you to reflect on how you can implement the book's ideas in your own contexts. We acknowledge that the future demands leaders who are not only visionary but also adaptable.

Leading for tomorrow's schools is not without its challenges. As we look ahead, we must acknowledge the inevitable shifts in technology, demographics, and societal expectations that will continue to impact our schools. Emerging technologies will require leaders to be more adaptive than ever. Changing student demographics will require new approaches to equity, inclusion, and personalized learning. By using the CHANGE and Satir frameworks, we encourage you to embrace these changes as opportunities rather than obstacles.

School leaders of the future will need to be prepared to manage evolving complexities, and the insights shared in this book are intended to offer a pathway to effectively navigate these turbulent waters. Keep these tools as living frameworks that evolve as new challenges arise, and remember that embracing a growth mindset will help ensure your leadership remains relevant and impactful.

We need to be or become leaders who are able to navigate the complexities of change while remaining anchored in the core values that define educational excellence. Throughout this book, we've delved into the importance of change and growth planning, emphasizing that leadership is not a static role but a dynamic process that requires foresight, resilience, and a commitment to continuous improvement.

As we shared in the Preface, "To be clear, we are telling the stories of our people. We may have created the conditions, nudged, or supported the change process, but the credit goes where it is due: our faculty, staff, students, communities, and Boards of Education." Leadership is a team sport!

The strategies outlined, from cultivating a culture of collaboration to leveraging data for informed decision-making, provide a roadmap for leaders seeking to drive meaningful change in their schools. Moreover, the CHANGE Leadership Framework shown in Figure C.1 introduced our research-influenced, evidence-based framework for leading for tomorrow's schools today.

- Challenge the Process
- Have Open Conversations
- Adapt and Be Flexible
- Navigate Obstacles
- Generate a Shared Vision
- Enjoy the Journey

This leadership framework serves as a guiding principle for leaders at all levels and across industries. Combined with the Satir Change Model and the case studies shared throughout the book, we demonstrate that we can create conditions for the next Johannes Gutenberg, and we can and must transform, for our youth and the future world depend on us to do so.

It helps to underscore the idea that leadership is not just about achieving goals but about inspiring and empowering others to contribute to a shared vision of success.

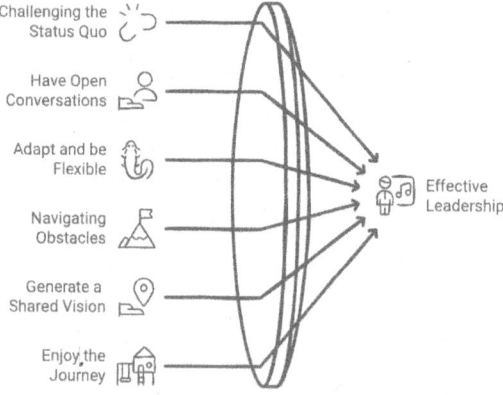

Figure C.1 CHANGE leadership framework. © Lubelfeld and Polyak.

In reflecting on the successes and challenges faced by North Shore School District 112 over the past several years, we see the tangible impact of strategic leadership. The district's achievements in elevating student voice, enhancing instructional practices, and fostering an inclusive culture of engagement offer valuable lessons for leaders everywhere. These accomplishments remind us that effective leadership is not just about managing the present but also about shaping the future with intentionality and purpose. Leadership is about the people served, not the people with leadership titles. Humility, an outstretched hand, and listening before talking will support tomorrow's schools every day.

The case study examples from Leyden High School District 212 also show how service to those being led and engagement with the partners in education shape their future. From the Co.Lab redesign of freshman year, to the pathways for students, to Teatro Leyden, the entire community is part of leading for tomorrow's schools today. What better solution is there to increase representation for the community than the Golden Ticket to bring the community back? Leading for tomorrow's schools today is not only possible, it's imperative.

As we look to the future, it is essential to recognize that the work of educational leadership is never truly finished. Throughout the book, we nod to earlier works, including *The Unlearning Leader*, and one of our books with P. J. Caposey, *The Unfinished Leader*. Those works underscore the foundations upon which our body of work is built.

The rapidly changing landscape of education, marked by technological advancements, evolving societal expectations, and the need for greater equity and inclusion, requires leaders who are willing to unlearn old habits and embrace new ways of thinking and doing. This process of unlearning and relearning is not a sign of weakness but a testament to the strength and courage required to lead in an ever-changing world. To that end, we're never truly finished; we never truly arrive; we iterate, reiterate, and become the next versions of ourselves (not the best versions of ourselves).

By framing each case study with the Satir Change Model, we acknowledge and show the challenges of change as well as the steps through which adaptive change can occur. As we show again in Figure C.2, this change model identifies that, when a change is introduced, the chaos/disequilibrium grows over time until a transformational event takes place,

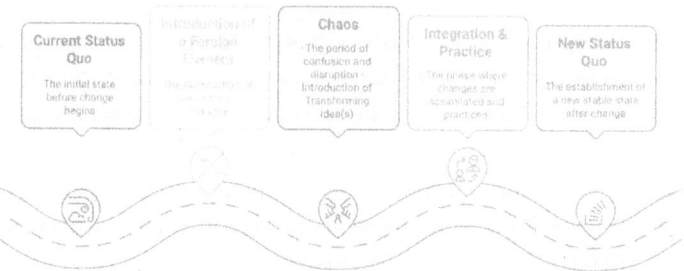

Figure C.2 Satir Change Model. Illustration by Michael Lubelfeld.

and the integration & practice of the change is accepted, and a new status quo is established.

By helping illustrate how to establish a new status quo, we show change and integration of practice are possible and impactful. Integrating Satir and our CHANGE frameworks pave the way on your roadmap for replicable change.

The voices from the field exemplify leadership from all over the nation in various ways of leading for tomorrow's schools today. In his foreword, Thomas C. Murray emphasizes the urgent need for educational leaders to navigate the complexities of today's rapidly changing world with trust, empathy, and innovation at the core of their leadership. Highlighting the practical frameworks and real-world insights offered in *Leading for Tomorrow's Schools Today*, he calls on educators to break free from traditional constraints, make bold decisions, and actively cultivate a culture of trust to prepare future-ready learners for a world that is constantly evolving.

In his essay, Glenn Robbins describes how Brigantine Public School District in New Jersey has navigated the challenges of a VUCA world by implementing progressive strategies that foster innovation, adaptability, and real-world skills for students. Through initiatives like innovative scheduling, ungraded classes, esports, and community partnerships, the district has become a model of forward-thinking education, demonstrating the power of continuous improvement and collaboration.

The next voice from the field comes from a superintendent in California. Dr. Zandra Jo Galván's essay emphasizes her people-centered leadership philosophy, highlighting how building strong relationships and community partnerships have driven success in Greenfield USD and now guide her vision for Salinas UHSD. By fostering trust, collaboration, and a shared commitment to student empowerment, she has implemented transformative initiatives like the Graduate Profile and strategic digital equity efforts, demonstrating the power of relationships to create sustainable, positive change in education.

Then we learned from New York superintendent and past president of the AASA, Dr. Gladys Cruz. In her essay, Gladys advocates for expanding educational pathways that go beyond traditional college preparatory programs, emphasizing the need for hands-on, real-world learning experiences to prepare students for diverse career opportunities. Through initiatives like Questar III BOCES' STEM high schools, career and technical education (CTE) programs, and New Visions bridge programs, she demonstrates how a focus on skills development, adaptability, and partnerships can better equip students to thrive in an evolving workforce and society.

Our final voice from the field is from Idaho superintendent Jeff Dillon. Jeff Dillon's essay emphasizes the need for a fundamental shift away from traditional, adult-centered education models toward a personalized, student-centered approach that empowers students as co-authors of their learning journey. Through the implementation of a "Student Bill of Rights," his district has established a framework to resist the pull back to outdated practices, ensuring that educational innovation remains focused on individual mastery, self-advocacy, and future-ready skills.

In closing, we encourage all educational leaders to approach their roles with a sense of optimism and possibility. The challenges ahead are significant, but so too are the opportunities to make a lasting impact. By staying true to our values, fostering a culture of innovation, and remaining committed to the growth and development of both ourselves and our teams, we can lead our schools into a future that is not only brighter but also more just, equitable, and inclusive for all students.

This is not just a book to be read, but a guide to be lived. Use these tools to actively create environments where students, educators, and communities can thrive. We have seen firsthand the transformative power of courageous leadership, and we hope you will use these lessons to inspire your teams and drive meaningful change.

When we started this book, we discussed navigating the unpredictable waters of educational leadership. Just like Johannes Gutenberg's printing press revolutionized the world by providing access to information, we believe that embracing change today can revolutionize the future of our students. With the tools and insights provided, we hope you now feel better equipped to guide your own ship, charting a course that leads not only to success for your students but also to a sustainable and flourishing future for your schools.

Remember, the future is not something to be passively awaited—it is something we build, decision by decision, day by day. So grab the CHANGE Leadership Framework, and lead your schools to where they need to be. The future is waiting for you.

Appendix A
Interviews from the Pandemic Era—Use Case for Generative AI and Leadership

School leadership during the pandemic is the adaptive challenge of all time.
—Deborah Jewell-Sherman, Harvard Professor

In this appendix, we share evidence of adaptive and transformational leadership during the unprecedented Covid-19 worldwide pandemic. We share leadership lessons as well as the integrative use of generative artificial intelligence tools that allowed us to take hours of audio content and distill it into this section of the book.

In the context of the book *Leading for Tomorrow's Schools Today*, we take a generative artificial intelligence tool, TurboScribe, and we transcribe audio interviews (podcasts and video interviews from the authors). We then take the transcripts, and using OpenAI's ChatGPT 4.0, create content for the book.

For context, the purposes of this appendix are threefold:

1. Acknowledgment of the transformative impact of the pandemic-era leadership on us and the impact on public education
2. Demonstration of an additional Gen AI use case for leadership and complex data analysis/synthesis
3. Remembering that we collectively adapted, pivoted, and transformed far more rapidly than we would have ever imagined—and our focus was always on the general welfare and well-being of our kids, staff, and the community.

This quote at the start of the appendix underscores the unprecedented challenges faced by school leaders during the pandemic and highlights the need for adaptive approaches in education. In March 2020, the world, including our nation and schools, faced the profound impacts of the Covid-19 pandemic and ensuing shutdowns. The presented content in this appendix reflects on the priorities of humanity and the adaptive leadership lessons from these unprecedented experiences. The authors, in their leadership practice, focused on social, emotional, survival, and Maslow needs first and foremost before delving into e-learning programming.

As we have done throughout the book, we offer you reflective questions for contemplation, review, and ultimate action:

- What were the most adaptive changes your organization demonstrated during the pandemic that are still in place today?
- How did your priorities change during the pandemic's challenges?
- In what ways are you addressing student learning, chronic absenteeism, and mental health needs post-pandemic?
- In what ways did your approaches to work change as a result of living and leading through the pandemic?

Before we dive into the actual content and leadership lessons, we want to share the "why" for using Turbo Scribe and ChatGPT to produce the messages in this appendix. A large part of the content was generated via the use and application of the generative artificial intelligence tools Turbo Scribe and OpenAI's ChatGPT 4.0.

During the pandemic period, as regional leaders, we participated in a number of audio and video interviews. One way for you, the reader, to engage with that content would be to listen to the interviews. This would take about six hours of real time. That content, and that duration, might be inaccessible, but the content is germane, and we wanted a way to take that volume and synthesize it (using Gen AI tools) for integration into this manuscript. For reference, transcript summaries of the interviews (TurboScribe converted the audio into text) are shared later in this appendix.

Beyond simply taking the hours of audio content and using Turbo Scribe to get transcripts and re-publishing as is here, we took the additional step to apply Gen AI to our practice as another illustration of its power and utility. We prompted ChatGPT to do "something" with the content, and we're sharing highlights with you here!

This is another way we seek to tell our stories and share lessons from the field with you! Before we share the analysis and synthesis of interview content, we'll begin by applying the overall adaptive leadership experience from the Covid-19 era via the Satir Model of Change:

- *Current Status Quo* (March 2020)—Every sector of life and the economy was normal until March 2020, when it wasn't. Some school districts were 1:1 with devices, but very few were doing any online or remote learning. No one had ever considered the idea of wearing a mask inside a school building.

- *Introduction of a Foreign Element*—The last time there was a worldwide global pandemic was the Spanish Flu of 1918. No one really had any preparation for how to deal with this on such a scale. We thought we might be closed for a few days or a few weeks and then go back to normal.

- *Chaos*—All of a sudden, educators were expected to be health care decision-makers. Nurses were swabbing noses, students were spitting into tubes, and pandemic politics showed up at our Board meetings. Government metrics and guidance were changing regularly. We needed to teach kids remotely and feed kids remotely. We were content providers, Wi-Fi providers, and device providers. It was chaos on every level.

- *Integration*—There was the immediate integration of e-learning. It wasn't ideal, it wasn't all great, but we did it. We did things educationally that we would never have thought possible. We built capacity while building empathy. Teachers saw right into their students' homes and vice versa. Words like synchronous and asynchronous became commonplace as we reinvented education on the fly.

- *New Status Quo*—We have endured a (hopefully) once-in-a-lifetime worldwide global pandemic. In that, we have experienced that immediate and profound adaptability can take place. We also learned how to take the leadership lessons and take affirmative steps to prevent exacerbating inequities that were unearthed and spotlighted as a result of the Covid-19 experiences. We are now better prepared for whatever lies ahead.

As promised, here is a sampling of our words, transcribed and repackaged by Gen AI:

Impact of the Pandemic

The mission of our school districts remained the same: to provide support for our communities and students. However, the mechanism of delivery transformed overnight. Despite the buildings being closed, school continued across the country.

Adapting to New Realities

We needed to rethink student-teacher interactions, social-emotional needs, and meal provisions. Leadership roles expanded beyond traditional figures like school board members, district administrators, and teacher leaders. Teachers transformed their practices, and counselors and social workers addressed unique social-emotional needs. Coaches maintained connections with athletes, helping them navigate lost experiences.

Addressing Equity and Access

Equity remained a significant concern. Schools across the country struggled with students not engaging in their work due to various reasons. The pandemic brought to light the need for universal internet access, as devices without Wi-Fi were little more than expensive paperweights. This highlighted the existing digital divide and necessitated efforts to bridge this gap.

Equity issues became more apparent as we shifted to remote learning. Challenges included students being home alone, caring for siblings, or contributing to family income. The need for universal internet access became clear, as devices without Wi-Fi were useless.

Understanding equity from the perspective of those receiving the support was crucial. Providing devices and internet access alone was not sufficient; it was essential to understand the unique needs and circumstances of each family and student.

Reimagining Milestone Events

We also had to rethink milestone events, like graduations and awards nights, and ensure clear communication with stakeholders. The pandemic highlighted both the best and worst of our educational system. Communities rallied to support each other, while existing inequities became more transparent.

Unsung Heroes

Our doctors, nurses, and first responders became even bigger community heroes. Similarly, our cafeteria workers, cooks, bus drivers, and maintenance staff continued to support our students, often working in person to support our students.

In every setting, guiding missions and philosophies, such as student voice and teacher voice, became crucial. Schools needed to prioritize psychological needs, following Maslow's hierarchy, before addressing educational needs outlined in Bloom's Taxonomy.

Leadership Lessons and Innovations

The Covid-19 pandemic required swift adaptation, innovation, and a focus on both immediate and long-term solutions. Leaders prioritized basic needs, social-emotional health, and clear communication.

Social-Emotional Support

The social-emotional well-being of students and staff became a critical priority. Recognizing that everyone reacts differently to stress and change, we ensured that mental health resources were available and accessible. This involved addressing the diverse needs of our communities during these challenging times, and providing counselors and social workers to support students dealing with anxiety, fear, and other emotional challenges.

Communication Strategies

Clear and effective communication was crucial. Regular, transparent communication kept everyone informed and engaged. Various methods, such as video messages and concise emails, ensured the community was aware of the steps being taken and the reasons behind them. This transparency helped build trust and manage expectations, which were essential in maintaining a sense of stability and reassurance.

Adaptive Leadership and E-Learning (E-Learning Is "Computer-Based Instruction")

One of the first and foremost priorities during the pandemic was ensuring the basic needs of students and families were met. In our respective districts, we emphasized the importance of feeding students, shifting operations to provide thousands of meals daily. This focus on basic needs ensured that no child went hungry and highlighted the fundamental role schools play in supporting their communities.

The pandemic necessitated a rapid shift to e-learning and remote learning. Leaders identified this as a key priority, working to maximize academic opportunities despite the challenges. Adaptability and continuous improvement were essential, constantly refining approaches to ensure effective learning. Teachers transformed family rooms, home offices, and even garages into makeshift live-streaming video studios.

Collaboration and Unity

Collaboration and unity were essential. Leaders highlighted the importance of working together, involving various stakeholders in the decision-making processes. This inclusive approach fostered a supportive and engaged community, allowing for more effective problem-solving and implementation of new strategies.

Future Preparedness

The Covid-19 experiences emphasized the need to prepare for future challenges. Leaders acknowledged that new challenges would continue to arise. Resilience and adaptability were crucial, preparing for future challenges by continuously improving and iterating on approaches.

Long-Term Solutions

A significant takeaway was the focus on long-term solutions over short-term fixes. The pandemic provided an opportunity to make lasting changes that would benefit students and teachers in the long run. Leaders aimed to address systemic issues and create sustainable solutions that would continue to support educational growth and equity.

Recreating reality instead of returning to the old normal was a key focus. The pandemic highlighted that "normal" was not effective for many, and this period of disruption offered a chance to redefine educational practices for the better.

Flexible Learning Options and Non-Traditional Work Hours

Creating flexible learning options, such as an online learning academy, was discussed. This approach can accommodate various family situations and reduce trauma by maintaining connectivity and continuity in education.

Exploring non-traditional work hours and roles for staff to better support students and families was highlighted. Flexibility in staff schedules, such as having family engagement specialists available during non-traditional hours, can meet the diverse needs of students, especially those living in poverty.

Supporting Students in Poverty

Recognizing and addressing the unique needs of students living in poverty is crucial. Poverty often involves trauma and irregular work hours, requiring schools to adapt their support systems to be more responsive and flexible.

Family Engagement

Taking advantage of the increased connection with families due to virtual learning has opened new opportunities for engagement and support. Schools should maximize the benefits of this connection to enhance learning and community involvement.

Redesigning the School Day

Redesigning the school day to be more flexible and engaging was emphasized. Providing holistic, 360-degree support to students ensures they receive the help they need when they need it most.

Holistic Support Systems

Implementing holistic support systems that cater to students' diverse needs was advocated. A comprehensive approach to student support, addressing both academic and nonacademic needs, fosters overall wellbeing and success.

Future-Oriented Education

Building toward a future-oriented education system was stressed. The pandemic provided a glimpse of the future, and schools need to leverage this experience to make meaningful improvements that will help them thrive in the long term.

Guiding Principles

Establishing clear guiding principles to navigate challenges helped maintain a coherent and focused approach throughout the pandemic. Safety, learning, and communication were the core principles that guided decision-making.

Empowering Principals

Empowering principals as CEOs of their buildings allowed for more responsive and adaptive leadership. Giving principals autonomy to make decisions based on their knowledge of their students, parents, and school facilities fostered a culture of shared leadership.

Professional Growth and Development

Investing in professional growth and development was highlighted. Continuous learning for leaders and helping principals and staff grow through professional development opportunities were essential for maintaining effective leadership.

Building Capacity

Building capacity and empowering others within the organization helped create a culture of shared leadership and continuous improvement. Enabling leaders to act and lead in their own settings was crucial for effective leadership.

Returning to Fundamentals

Returning to fundamentals and core values during challenging times helped leaders stay grounded. Remembering the "why" behind their work and seeking help and support when needed were essential.

Collaboration with Health Departments

Collaboration with local and state health departments and other educational leaders provided valuable resources and support during the pandemic. This network helped guide decision-making and the implementation of new strategies.

Student-Centered Learning

Focusing on student-centered learning and creating personalized opportunities for students helped address individual needs and promote their passions.

Leading with Humility

Leading with humility and kindness was essential. Recognizing that leadership is about facilitating and supporting others rather than imposing one's will helped create a supportive and collaborative environment.

Driving Change Proactively

Embracing and driving change proactively helped leaders transition smoothly during the pandemic. Forward-thinking approaches and innovative practices were key to navigating the challenges.

Simplifying Communication

Simplifying communication and mission statements made it easier for everyone to remember and act upon. Clear, concise communication helped maintain focus and understanding.

Enhancing Learning with Technology

Utilizing technology to enhance learning and engagement was crucial. Implementing one-to-one devices and digital platforms facilitated remote learning and supported education.

Viewing the Crisis as an Opportunity

Viewing the crisis as an opportunity for growth helped leaders adopt new practices and highlight the potential for ongoing improvement.

> Embracing lessons learned during the pandemic can lead to lasting positive changes in education.mode_comment

As mentioned, we prompted ChatGPT to take our content from above and show how the content from this Appendix A, originally entitled, "So We Were in a Pandemic" aligns with our CHANGE Leadership Framework:

C—Challenge the Process: The pandemic was an unprecedented challenge that required school leaders to rethink and challenge every aspect of their processes. Traditional methods of teaching, communication, and support were upended, forcing leaders to innovate and find new ways to fulfill their mission. The shift to remote learning, the need for universal internet access, and the reimagining of milestone events like graduations were all ways in which leaders challenged and transformed their established processes.

H—Have Open Conversations: During the pandemic, open conversations became vital. Leaders needed to maintain transparent and honest communication with all stakeholders—teachers, students, parents, and the broader community. These conversations were essential for building trust, managing expectations, and ensuring that everyone understood the reasons behind difficult decisions, such as school closures and shifts to remote learning. The emphasis on clear, effective communication strategies is a direct reflection of the importance of keeping dialogue open and inclusive.

A—Adapt and Be Flexible: Adaptability and flexibility were at the core of pandemic leadership. School leaders had to quickly adapt to the new reality of remote education, addressing not only academic needs but also social-emotional support and basic needs like food security. Flexibility in roles, work hours, and learning environments became crucial as leaders worked to meet the diverse needs of their communities. This flexibility also extended to long-term changes, as leaders began to implement lasting solutions that would continue to benefit students and educators beyond the pandemic.

N—Navigate Obstacles: The pandemic presented numerous obstacles that required careful navigation. From addressing the digital divide to ensuring the well-being of students and staff, leaders had to find ways to overcome these challenges while staying true to their mission. This involved collaborating with health departments, leveraging technology, and developing new strategies for continuous learning and support. Effective navigation required not only strategic thinking but also the ability to remain calm and resilient in the face of uncertainty.

G—Generate a Shared Vision: In the midst of the pandemic's chaos, generating a shared vision became more important than ever. Leaders needed to bring their communities together around a common purpose, ensuring that everyone was working toward the same goals despite the many political and ideological challenges. This shared vision included a commitment to equity, continuous improvement, and the well-being of students and staff. By focusing on long-term solutions and reimagining what education could look like post-pandemic, leaders helped their communities see beyond the immediate crisis and work toward a better future.

E—Enjoy the Journey: Despite the difficulties, leaders were encouraged to enjoy the journey and find meaning in the challenges they faced. The pandemic was an opportunity for growth, innovation, and the development of new skills. By maintaining a positive attitude and celebrating the small victories along the way, leaders were able to stay motivated and inspire others to do the same. This focus on resilience and positivity helped create a sense of purpose and fulfillment, even in the most trying times.

Applying the CHANGE model to the leadership strategies we employed and learned about from colleagues around the world during the Covid-19 pandemic reveals a comprehensive approach to transforming education. Their emphasis on equity, innovation, and resilience provides a robust framework for leading schools toward a better and more flexible future.

Recall that a great deal of the content of this chapter came from "in-time" interviews that we engaged in to give you a real recap of our actions and models. In addition, we added some content, context, and post-Covid analysis so that we can continue to learn from experience and lead for tomorrow's schools today. We don't lament the pandemic; we learn from it!

Our youth deserve unprecedented leadership! They deserve equitable access to the best educational opportunities! They deserve, and society deserves, for their education to be maximized.

Leading through the Covid-19 pandemic required adaptability, innovation, and a focus on both immediate and long-term solutions. By prioritizing basic needs, social-emotional health, effective communication, collaboration, and continuous improvement, leaders have demonstrated how to transform challenges into opportunities for growth and improvement in education. Their holistic approach, emphasizing equity, empathy, and resilience, provides a roadmap for leading schools toward a better and more flexible future.

As you reflect on your own experiences during the pandemic, we bring you back to those reflective questions to consider the adaptive changes your organization made and how those changes continue to impact student learning and mental health post-pandemic. It encourages leaders to embrace the lessons learned during this time, viewing the crisis as an opportunity to drive meaningful change in education.

Before we list out the interview transcripts for reference, it's time to revisit those reflective questions:

- What were the most adaptive changes your organization demonstrated during the pandemic that are still in place today?
- How did your priorities change during the pandemic's challenges?
- In what ways are you addressing student learning, chronic absenteeism, and mental health needs post-pandemic?
- In what ways did your approaches to work change as a result of living and leading through the pandemic?

Summaries of Podcast Interviews

https://bit.ly/DisruptEdVlog

The Disrupt Education Vlog can be found on YouTube to hear it in podcast form. Here are some distilled leadership lessons from Mike Lubelfeld and Nick Polyak during the Covid-19 pandemic:

1. Adaptability and Innovation:

    Embrace a culture of continuous improvement and innovation. Both leaders highlighted the importance of being open to new ideas and creative solutions. For example, Mike Lubelfeld mentioned the importance of being agile and making iterative improvements, while Nick Polyak emphasized building a culture of unlearning and innovation within the school district.

2. Resilience and Positivity:

Maintain a resilient and positive attitude. Both leaders emphasized the importance of staying energized and motivated despite challenges. They highlighted how their staff and communities adapted to the new realities brought by the pandemic with creativity and resilience.

3. Community and Collaboration:

Engage with the community and foster collaboration. Both Mike and Nick talked about the importance of listening to teachers, students, and parents and involving them in decision-making processes. This inclusive approach helps build a supportive and engaged community.

4. Student-Centered Approaches:

Focus on student-centered learning. Nick Polyak shared an example of creating Extended Learning Opportunities (ELO) to help students recover credits in a personalized manner, demonstrating the importance of addressing individual student needs and promoting their passions.

5. Leadership and Humility:

Lead with humility and kindness. Mike Lubelfeld emphasized the need for leaders to remain humble, kind, and open to listening to others. Recognizing that leadership is about facilitating and supporting others rather than imposing one's will is crucial for effective leadership.

6. Embracing Change:

Embrace and drive change proactively. Both leaders highlighted how they had already been pushing for innovative practices, such as e-learning and one-to-one device initiatives, even before the pandemic. This forward-thinking approach helped them transition more smoothly when the pandemic hit.

7. Clear and Simple Communication:

Simplify communication and mission statements. Both leaders emphasized the importance of clear, concise communication. Mike shared how they distilled their district's mission statement into three key words: inspire, innovate, engage , making it easier for everyone to remember and act upon.

8. Focus on Well-Being:

Prioritize the well-being of students and staff. Mike highlighted the importance of ensuring that students have access to meals and other essential services during school closures. This focus on well-being helps build a supportive and caring school environment.

9. Leveraging Technology :

    Utilize technology to enhance learning and engagement. Nick Polyak discussed the successful implementation of one-to-one devices and the use of digital platforms to facilitate remote learning, underscoring the importance of leveraging technology to support education.

10. Learning from the Crisis:

    View the crisis as an opportunity for growth. Both leaders shared how the pandemic accelerated the adoption of new practices and highlighted the potential for ongoing improvement. Embracing the lessons learned during the pandemic can lead to lasting positive changes in education.

May 2020 Video with the American Association of School Administrators

https://bit.ly/AASAVideo

Here are the distilled leadership lessons from the interview with Mike Lubelfeld and Nick Polyak during the Covid-19 pandemic:

1. Prioritize Basic Needs:

    Ensure the basic needs of students and families are met first. Both leaders emphasized the importance of feeding students and their families, shifting operations to provide thousands of meals daily to ensure no child goes hungry.

2. Focus on Social-Emotional Health:

    Address the social-emotional well-being of students and staff. Nick highlighted the importance of taking care of everyone's mental health, recognizing that people react and respond differently during challenging times. Ensuring social-emotional support is a critical priority.

3. Effective Communication:

   Maintain clear and effective communication. Mike stressed the need for effective communication to keep everyone informed and engaged. This helps build trust and ensures that the community is aware of the steps being taken to support them.

4. Adapt to E-Learning:

   Focus on e-learning and remote learning. Both leaders identified e-learning as a key priority, working to maximize academic opportunities during the pandemic. This includes adapting teaching methods and ensuring students can continue their education remotely.

5. Collaborative Leadership:

   Emphasize the importance of collaboration and unity. Nick and Mike both highlighted that working together and staying united strengthens their ability to navigate challenges and support their communities effectively.

6. Comprehensive Support:

   Provide comprehensive support that addresses health, safety, and general welfare. Mike mentioned the need to account for the overall well-being of employees and students, ensuring their health and safety are prioritized alongside educational needs.

7. Prepare for Future Challenges:

   Stay resilient and prepare for future challenges. Both leaders acknowledged that new challenges will continue to arise, and it's essential to stay strong, adaptable, and ready to lead through them.

8. Community and Well-Being:

   Focus on the well-being of the entire community. Both leaders emphasized that their efforts are aimed not just at students but also at staff and the broader community. Ensuring the well-being of the whole community is crucial for overall success.

These lessons reflect a holistic approach to leadership during the pandemic, emphasizing the importance of meeting basic needs, supporting social-emotional health, effective communication, collaboration, and adaptability.

This Week in Education Podcast

https://bit.ly/ThisWeekInEducation

Here are the distilled leadership lessons from Mike Lubelfeld during his interview, focusing on leadership during the Covid-19 pandemic:

1. Long-Term Solutions over Short-Term Fixes:

    Focus on solving long-term problems in public education rather than just addressing immediate issues. Mike emphasized the importance of using this moment to create lasting changes in the education system.

2. Adapting to New Realities:

    Recreate reality instead of returning to the old normal. Mike pointed out that "normal" was not effective for many students and teachers, and the pandemic offers an opportunity to redefine educational practices for the better.

3. Leveraging Technology for Continuous Learning:

    Utilize technology to ensure continuous learning regardless of location. Mike highlighted how the pandemic has shown that learning can happen anywhere, whether on-site, virtually at home, or even in a hospital. This adaptability can benefit students with illnesses or other challenges that prevent them from attending school physically.

4. Student Flexibility and Online Learning:

    Consider creating flexible learning options, such as an online learning academy. Mike discussed the potential for fluid enrollment and multi-age, multi-grade online programs that can accommodate various family situations, military deployments, or personal tragedies, reducing trauma and maintaining connectivity.

5. Non-Traditional Work Hours and Roles:

    Explore non-traditional work hours and roles for staff to better support students and families. Mike mentioned the need for flexibility in staff schedules, such as having family engagement specialists or school social workers available during non-traditional hours to meet the diverse needs of students, especially those living in poverty.

6. Addressing Poverty and Trauma:

   Recognize and address the unique needs of students living in poverty. Mike emphasized that poverty often involves trauma and irregular work hours, requiring schools to adapt their support systems to be more responsive and flexible.

7. Maximizing Engagement in the Living Room:

   Take advantage of the increased connection with families due to virtual learning. Mike suggested that being in the living rooms of families has opened new opportunities for engagement and support, and schools should maximize the benefits of this connection.

8. Creating a More Flexible and Engaged School Day:

   Redesign the school day to be more flexible and engaging for students. Mike emphasized the need for schools to provide holistic, 360-degree support to students, ensuring they receive the help they need when they need it most.

9. Holistic Support Systems:

   Implement holistic support systems that cater to students' diverse needs. Mike advocated for a more comprehensive approach to student support, addressing both academic and nonacademic needs to foster overall well-being and success.

10. Future-Oriented Educational Practices:

    Build toward a future-oriented education system. Mike stressed that the pandemic has provided a glimpse of the future, and schools need to leverage this experience to make meaningful improvements that will help them thrive in the long term.

These lessons highlight the importance of adaptability, flexibility, and a focus on long-term improvements in education, emphasizing the need to address the unique challenges brought to light by the pandemic.

Future Ready Schools Podcast

https://bit.ly/FutureReadySchools

Here are the distilled leadership lessons from Mike Lubelfeld during the Covid-19 pandemic, based on his interview with Tom Murray:

1. Equity through the Lens of the Recipient:

   Understand equity from the perspective of those receiving the support. Mike emphasized the importance of looking at equity through the lens of the learner and their family, acknowledging that providing devices and internet access alone is not sufficient. It's essential to understand the unique needs and circumstances of each family and student.

2. Guiding Principles:

   Establish clear guiding principles to navigate challenges. Mike highlighted how his district focused on safety, learning, and communication as their core guiding principles, which helped them maintain a coherent and focused approach throughout the pandemic.

3. Collaborative Leadership:

   Foster a collaborative leadership team. Mike praised his leadership team for their dedication, creativity, and flexibility. He emphasized the importance of a project management approach, involving various departments and stakeholders to tackle challenges together.

4. Empowering Principals:

   Empower principals as CEOs of their buildings. Mike advocated for giving principals the autonomy to make decisions based on their knowledge of their students, parents, and school facilities. This empowerment helps create a responsive and adaptive leadership culture.

5. Adaptability and Continuous Improvement:

   Embrace adaptability and continuous improvement. Mike described how his team constantly ideated, executed, monitored, and refined their approaches. This iterative process allowed them to adapt to changing circumstances effectively.

6. Clear and Concise Communication:

Prioritize clear and concise communication. Mike emphasized the importance of coherent leadership and clear communication. He discussed using various communication methods, such as video messages and concise emails, to ensure the community stays informed and engaged.

7. Professional Growth and Development:

    Invest in professional growth and development. Mike stressed the importance of continuous learning for leaders, mentioning his involvement with AASA and the importance of helping principals and staff grow through professional development opportunities.

8. Leading with Empathy:

    Lead with empathy and understanding. Mike discussed the importance of listening to teachers, students, and parents with genuine empathy. He emphasized that leaders should truly understand the perspectives, fears, hopes, and celebrations of their community members.

9. Addressing Equity Issues:

    Actively address equity issues highlighted by the pandemic. Mike provided an example of how his district addressed chronic truancy by bringing disconnected children back to school to facilitate remote learning. He underscored the need for authentic and honest efforts to provide equitable access to education.

10. Building Capacity and Empowering Others:

    Build capacity and empower others. Mike talked about the importance of enabling and empowering leaders within the organization to act and lead in their settings. This approach helps create a culture of shared leadership and continuous improvement.

11. Focus on Fundamentals and Core Values:

    Return to fundamentals and core values. Mike advised leaders to reset and focus on their fundamental principles and core values, especially during challenging times. He encouraged leaders to remember their "why" and seek help and support when needed.

12. Community and Support:

Build a supportive community. Mike highlighted the importance of seeking help from the board and other leaders. He stressed the value of having a community of leaders who support each other and work together toward a common goal.

These lessons reflect Mike Lubelfeld's approach to leading through unprecedented times, emphasizing equity, collaboration, communication, empathy, and continuous improvement.

Based on the transcript from the interview with Franczek, the leadership strategies and priorities emphasized by Mike Lubelfeld and Nick Polyak during the Covid-19 pandemic align well with the key points previously summarized. Here are the main areas of focus they discussed:

1. Early and Collaborative Planning:

    Both superintendents highlighted the significance of early decision-making and planning. They initiated discussions with teachers' unions and other stakeholders to collaboratively plan for scenarios like remote and hybrid learning models.

2. Communication and Transparency:

    Mike and Nick emphasized the importance of regular and transparent communication. They aimed to keep all stakeholders informed about decisions, the rationale behind them, and any updates or changes. This communication helped maintain trust and manage expectations.

3. Adaptation and Flexibility:

    They discussed significant adaptations to school operations and teaching methods. For instance, Nick mentioned Leyden High School District's shift to a modified block schedule to simplify virtual learning and reduce the workload for both students and teachers.

4. Emphasis on Safety and Public Health Guidance:

    Ensuring safety by adhering to public health guidelines and collaborating with local health departments was a priority. They made adjustments based on evolving public health information to ensure the safety of students and staff.

5. Support for Students and Staff:

Both superintendents acknowledged the challenges faced by students, families, and staff, such as accessing suitable learning environments and mental health support. They made efforts to accommodate various needs, including providing spaces within schools for students who could not engage in remote learning from home.

6. Engagement with Legal and Educational Guidelines:

    They navigated the legal and educational guidelines that were rapidly evolving. This involved staying updated with state and federal educational policies and integrating them into their districts' operational plans.

7. Unlearning and Relearning:

    Both leaders discussed the concept of "unlearning" outdated practices and beliefs to adapt to new realities. They emphasized the need to unlearn traditional schooling methods and adopt flexible, innovative approaches to education during the pandemic.

8. Delegation and Team Management:

    They spoke about delegating responsibilities effectively and trusting their teams. Both superintendents emphasized the importance of distributive leadership, allowing various team members to take on leadership roles and responsibilities to manage the workload efficiently.

9. Use of Technology and Virtual Tools:

    They utilized technology and virtual tools to facilitate communication and learning. Regular virtual meetings, video messages, and online resources were employed to keep the school community connected and informed.

10. Collaboration with Local and State Leadership:

    Mike and Nick praised the support and guidance from local and state health departments, as well as their collaboration with other superintendents and educational leaders. This network provided valuable resources and support during the pandemic.

Overall, the transcript supports the previous summary, demonstrating how Mike and Nick effectively led their districts through the challenges of the Covid-19 pandemic by prioritizing early planning, transparent communication, flexibility, safety, and collaboration.

Appendix B
AI in Education: Opportunities and Challenges

Teach AI shares foundational ideas for AI in education, including the following policy ideas: foster leadership, promote AI literacy, provide guidance, build capacity, and support innovation.

- AI is already used in schools and by students; therefore, clear policies and guidance are required to realize the benefits and mitigate the risks.
- AI should augment human capabilities, not replace them.
- Promoting AI literacy can help prepare students for the challenges of today's world and help them navigate an uncertain future.
- "It is imperative to address AI in education now to realize key opportunities, prevent and mitigate emergent risks, and tackle unintended consequences." (US Department of Education, May 2023).

How Will AI Impact the Economy and Workforce?

- Almost 40 percent of global jobs will be complemented or replaced by AI. (IMF, January 2024)
- AI may impact about 60 percent of jobs in advanced economies. (IMF, January 2024)
- The skills required to succeed in jobs will change by 65 percent by 2030. (LinkedIn, November 2023)

What Are the Risks of AI in Education, and How Can We Mitigate Them?

- To reduce the effects of bias and misinformation in AI tools, we need to teach students how to critically assess AI content and create a robust public infrastructure that enhances bias testing and transparency. It is a shared responsibility.
- Policies should address existing inequities and digital divides.
- Important decisions should always involve a human with the final authority and responsibility for making those decisions, ensuring a "human is in the loop."

Teach AI (and Others) Recommend the Following:

Promote AI Literacy

- As AI becomes more common in education and the workforce, teaching AI literacy's human and technological aspects is crucial to preparing students for the future.
- Integrating AI literacy into academic standards and instruction creates informed consumers and future creators of AI-powered technologies.
- Promoting AI literacy in schools will help students be competitive in the future workforce.

Provide Guidance

- AI in schools presents new challenges in data privacy and security, academic integrity, bullying, and harassment—adding to the myriad of issues already facing schools.
- Policymakers must equip schools with comprehensive guidance to ensure AI's safe, responsible, and effective use in the classroom.

Build Capacity

- Policymakers can build system-wide capacity by providing opportunities to develop AI literacy.

- Investing in educator and staff professional development builds system-wide capacity and empowers schools to teach with and about AI.

Support Innovation

- AI in education has potential benefits and risks. We must track, study, and evaluate its use to ensure its effectiveness.

- Funding research and development on AI in education can help educators and staff make well-informed, evidence-based decisions.

Figure B.1 (from the US Department of Education) emphasizes the importance of humans, people, and relationships. Generative AI is a tool to enhance our work and service for children! No humans will be replaced as a result of the exploration of the viability and integration of generative AI tools in our system. However, because the nature of jobs will change, humans will need to adapt to our necessity in different ways.

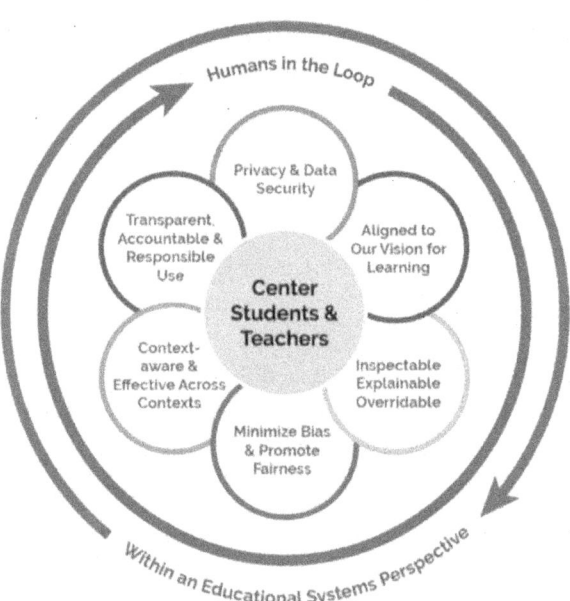

Figure B.1 What is Artificial Intelligence? *Source:* US Department of Education Office of Technology, based on Regona et al. (2022).

Appendix C
Generative Artificial Intelligence Tools Used Throughout This Book and NSSD 112 Board Policy Information

OpenAI—ChatGPT
Google's Gemini
Claude
TurboScribe
Magic School AI
Copilot
Google's Notebook LM
Latimer
Khanmigo
Curipod
Claude
Brisk
Teach AI
School AI
Eduaide
Stretch AI
Invideo
Hey Gen

NSSD 112
Board Policy Information—Reference

6:40 – Curriculum Development

6:210 – Instructional Materials

6:235 – Access to Electronic Networks

7:190 – Student Behavior

7:345 – Use of Educational Technologies; Student Data Privacy and Security

References

Anti-Defamation League. "Online Hate and Harassment: The American Experience 2023." Accessed October 30, 2024. https://www.adl.org/resources/report/online-hate-and-harassment-american-experience-2023.

Anti-Defamation League. "What Is Swatting?" Accessed October 30, 2024. https://www.adl.org/resources/article/what-swatting.

Black, Brad. *Talent, Culture, and Teams: The eX Factors of Excellence*. Independently Published, Streamline Books, 2024.

Brown, L. *Culture of Love: Cultivating a Positive and Transformational Organizational Culture*. Rochester, NY: WGW Publishing, Inc., 2018.

Casas, J. *Live Your Excellence*. San Diego, CA: Dave Burgess Consulting, Inc., 2020.

Clear, James. *Atomic Habits: An Easy & Proven Way to Build Good Habits & Break Bad Ones*. New York: Penguin (Avery), 2018.

Collins, J. *Good to Great*. New York, NY: Harper Collins, 2001.

Couros, G. *The Innovator's Mindset*. San Diego, CA: Dave Burgess Consulting, Inc., 2016.

Covey, S. L. *The Seven Habits of Highly Successful People*. New York, NY: Free Press, 1989.

Creasman, B., B. Futrell, and T. Rubin. *ConnectED Leaders: Network and Amplify Your Superintendency*. Lanham, MD: Rowman & Littlefield, 2019.

Dahl, Roald. 1971. *Willy Wonka & the Chocolate Factory*. Directed by Mel Stuart. Los Angeles: Paramount Pictures.

Dweck, Carol S. *Mindset: The New Psychology of Success*. New York: Ballantine Books, 2006.

EdWeek: "A Survey Conducted by Merrimack College in Partnership with Education Week found that 35% of Teachers Are Fairly likely to Leave the Profession within the Next Two Years"1. EdWeekhttps://www.edweek.org/research-center/reports/teaching-profession-in-crisis-national-teacher-survey

English, Fenwick W., and Lisa Ehrich. *Leading Beautifully: Educational Leadership as Connoisseurship*. New York: Routledge, 2016.

Fadel, Charles, Andrew Black, Robert Taylor, John Slesinski, and Kathleen Dunne. *Education for the Age of AI*. Boston, MA: The Center for Curriculum Redesign, 2024.

Fenwick, L. *Jim Crow's Pink Slip: The Untold Story of Black Principal and Teacher Leadership*. Cambridge, MA: Harvard University Press, 2022.

Fitzgerald, F. Scott. *The Great Gatsby*. Ware, England: Wordsworth Editions, 2019.

Fullan, Michael, and Mary Jean Gallagher. *The Devil is in the Details: System Solutions for Equity, Excellence, and Student Well-Being*. Thousand Oaks, CA: Corwin Press, 2020.

Fullan, Michael, and Joanne Quinn. *The Drivers: Transforming Learning for Students, Schools, and Systems*. Thousand Oaks, CA: Corwin Press, 2024.

Gallup. "Q12 Employee Engagement Survey." Retrieved from Gallup, 2023.

Gallup: Gallup's Perspective on Understanding the K–12 Teacher Experience. Retrieved from https://www.utah.gov/pmn/files/1186113.pdf.

Geography of Illinois, retrieved from Geography of Illinois – Wikipedia

Glanton, Dahleen. "Highland Park Schools Crisis Escalates into 'Civil War.'" *Chicago Tribune*, April 15, 2016. https://www.chicagotribune.com/news/local/breaking/ct-highland-park-school-crisis-civil-war-20160415-story.html.

Hanson, Melanie. "U.S. Public Education Spending Statistics." *EducationData.org*, 2022. Retrieved from EducationData.org.

Hattie, J. *Visible Learning*. London: Routledge, 2008.

Hattie, J., and G. Yates. *Visible Learning and the Science of How We Learn*. New York, NY: Routledge, 2014.

John, Oliver P., and Sanjay Srivastava. "The Big Five Trait Taxonomy: History, Measurement, and Theoretical Perspectives." In *Handbook of Personality: Theory and Research*, edited by Lawrence A. Pervin and Oliver P. John, 2nd ed., 102–38. New York: Guilford Press, 1999.

Jukes, Ian, and Ted McCain. "Beyond TTWWADI: Reconsidering Education in the Information & Communication Age." The Info Savvy Group, 2007.

Khan, Sal. *The One World School House*. New York: Twelve, 2016.

Khan, Sal. *Brave New Words: How AI Will Revolutionize Education (And Why That's a Good Thing)*. New York: Viking, 2024.

Kennedy, John F. "Speech at the University of Chicago," June 6, 1957. In *Public Papers of the Presidents of the United States: John F. Kennedy, 1961–1963*, Washington, D.C.: U.S. Government Printing Office, 1964.

Kouzes, J. M., and B. Z. Posner. *The Leadership Challenge*, 5th ed. San Francisco, CA: Jossey-Bass, 2012.

Kurtz, Holly. "A Profession in Crisis: Results of the First Annual Merrimack College Teacher Survey." *Education Week*, April 14, 2022.

Li, Fei-Fei. *The Worlds I See: Curiosity, Exploration, and Discovery at the Dawn of AI*. New York: Macmillan, 2023.

Lubelfeld, Michael, and Nick Polyak. *The Unlearning Leader: Leading for Tomorrow's Schools Today*. Lanham, MD: Rowman & Littlefield, 2017.

Lubelfeld, Michael, Nick Polyak, and P. J. Caposey. *Student Voice: From Invisible to Invaluable*. Lanham, MD: Rowman & Littlefield, 2018.

Lubelfeld, Michael, Nick Polyak, and P. J. Caposey. *The Unfinished Leader: A School Leadership Framework for Growth & Development*. Lanham, MD: Rowman & Littlefield, 2021.

Lubelfeld, Michael, Nick Polyak, and P. J. Caposey. *The Unfinished Teacher: Becoming the Next Version of Yourself*. Lanham, MD: Rowman & Littlefield, 2023.

Marzano, Robert J., B. McNulty, and T. Waters. *School Leadership That Works*. Alexandria, VA: ASCD, 2005.

Merriam-Webster. "Definition of Innovation." Retrieved from Merriam-Webster Dictionary.

Mollick, Ethan. *Co-Intelligence: Living and Working with Artificial Intelligence*. New York: Portfolio, 2024.

Myers, I. B. *The Myers-Briggs Type Indicator: Manual (1962)*. Palo Alto, CA: Consulting Psychologists Press, 1962.

National Center for Education Statistics. "Eighty-six Percent of U.S. K-12 Public Schools Reported Challenges Hiring Teachers for the 2023-24 School Year, with 83 Percent Reporting Trouble Hiring for Non-Teacher Positions, Such as Classroom Aides, Transportation Staff, and Mental Health Professionals." https://nces.ed.gov/whatsnew/press_releases/10_17_2023.asp

National Education Association. "Beyond Burnout: What Must Be Done to Tackle Educator Shortage." Accessed June 30, 2024. https://nea.org.

O'Leary, John. *In Awe: Rediscover your Childlike Wonder to Unleash Inspiration, Meaning, and Joy*. New York, NY: Currency, 2020.

Polyak, Nick. "Expanding Your Learning Network via #SuptChat." *School Administrator*, September 2016.

Reeves, Douglas B. *From Leading to Succeeding: The Seven Elements of Effective Leadership in Education*. Bloomington, IN: Solution Tree Press, 2016.

Reeves, Douglas B. *Leading Change in Your School: How to Conquer Myths, Build Commitment, and Get Results*. Alexandria, VA: Association for Supervision and Curriculum Development, 2009.

Regona, Massimo, Tan Yigitcanlar, Bo Xia, and R.Y.M. Li. "Opportunities and Adoption Challenges of AI in the Construction Industry: A PRISMA Review." *Journal of Open Innovation: Technology, Market, and Complexity* 8, no. 45 (2022). https://doi.org/10.3390/joitmc8010045. Cited in Office of Educational Technology. *Artificial Intelligence and the Future of Teaching and Learning*, May 2023. https://tech.ed.gov/files/2023/05/ai-future-of-teaching-and-learning-report.pdf.

Robinson, K. "Changing Educational Paradigms." TED. Retrieved from TED, 2010.

Robinson, K. *Creative Schools: The Grassroots Revolution That's Transforming Education*. New York, NY: Viking Penguin, 2015.

Roosevelt, Theodore. "Do What You Can, with What You Have, Where You Are." In *Theodore Roosevelt's Letters to His Children*, edited by Joseph Bucklin Bishop. New York: Charles Scribner's Sons, 1919.

Sanfelippo, J. *Lead From Where You Are: Building Intention, Connection, and Direction in Our Schools*. San Diego, CA: IMPress, 2022.

Satir, Virginia. *The New Peoplemaking*. Mountain View, CA: Science and Behavior Books, 1988.

Schneider, J., and J. Berkshire. *A Wolf at the Schoolhouse Door*. New York City, NY: The New Press, 2020.

Sheninger, Eric, and Thomas C. Murray. *Learning Transformed: 8 Keys to Designing Tomorrow's Schools, Today*. Alexandria, VA: ASCD, 2017.

TeachAI. "Foundational Policy Ideas for AI in Education." 2024. Accessed May 8, 2024. https://teachai.org/policy.

Uldrich, Jack. "Unlearning Requires Some Situational Unawareness Training." November 2009. Retrieved from Unlearning Requires Some Situational Unawareness Training - Jack Uldrich.

United States Constitution. [Public Domain].

U.S. Office of Personnel Management. "Related Documents." Accessed October 30, 2024. http://apps.opm.gov/ADT/Content.aspx?page=RelatedDocuments.

Westman, L. *Student-Driven Differentiation: 8 Steps to Harmonize Learning in the Classroom*. Thousand Oaks, CA: Corwin Press, 2018.

Williams, K. *Ruthless Equity: Disrupt the Status Quo and Ensure Learning for ALL Students*. Atlanta, GA: Wish in One Hand Press, 2022.

Zhao, Yong. "Artificial Intelligence and Education: End the Grammar of Schooling." *ECNU Review of Education* 7, no. 3 (2024): 3–20.

About the Contributors

Dr. Gladys I. Cruz is the district superintendent of Questar III Board of Cooperative Educational Services (BOCES)—an intermediary education agency between the State Education Department and local districts. Questar III is one of thirty-seven BOCES across the state, expanding and enhancing educational opportunities to meet a diverse population of students. Students attend BOCES technical education programs, comprehensive high schools, senior-only high school to college bridge programs (New Visions), and specialized programs for exceptional children, in addition to adult education and pre-kindergarten programs. Questar III BOCES serves upstate New York's counties of Rensselaer, Columbia, and Greene in addition to districts statewide in a variety of service areas. She was the 2023–24 AASA President.

Jeff Dillon, Superintendent of Wilder School District in Idaho, is a visionary leader dedicated to transforming education through innovation and student-centered practices. With a career rooted in empowering rural schools, Jeff is recognized for his commitment to equity, personalized learning, and the integration of cutting-edge technology. His forward-thinking leadership has garnered statewide and national recognition, making Wilder School District a model for educational innovation.

Jeff's passion for creating opportunities extends beyond the classroom, as he collaborates with educators, policymakers, and communities to enhance learning experiences. Known for his ability to inspire and lead, Jeff continues to champion initiatives that prepare students for success in an ever-changing world while ensuring every learner thrives in a supportive environment.

Zandra Jo Galván, Superintendent of Salinas Union High School District in California, is a nationally recognized educational leader and advocate for equity and excellence. A proud past president of CALSA and treasurer of ALAS, Zandra was honored as the ALAS National Superintendent of the Year for 2023–24. She has also been named a Top 100 National Influencer by *District Administration* in 2024 and a DA Woman of Distinction in 2025.

With a career spanning over two decades, Zandra is celebrated for her transformative leadership, innovative practices, and commitment to empowering students and educators. A passionate mentor and speaker, she continues to inspire change and foster opportunities for success in every community she serves.

Glenn Robbins, Superintendent of Brigantine Public Schools in New Jersey, is a highly respected educator. With experience as a principal, assistant principal, teacher, and varsity coach, he is also the bestselling author of *Calm in the Chaos: Ancient Stoic Wisdom for Successful School Leadership*. Recognized internationally, Glenn's accolades include National Superintendent of the Year Finalist, NASSP Digital Principal of the Year, and NJ Visionary Superintendent Award. He has served on the AASA National Governing Board and Harvard Business Review Advisory Council. Invited to the White House and US Department of Education, Glenn inspires educational innovation, empowering students and educators to thrive in a VUCA world through equity, creativity, and leadership.

About the Authors

Michael Lubelfeld, EdD, currently serves as the superintendent of schools in the North Shore School District 112 in Highland Park, Illinois, a northern suburb of Chicago. Mike has been a superintendent in Illinois since 2010. He plans to retire from public service in 2026. Mike earned his doctor of education in curriculum and instruction from Loyola University of Chicago, where his published dissertation was on "Effective Instruction in Middle School Social Studies." He is also on the adjunct faculty at National Louis University in the Department of Educational Leadership. Mike has earned an IASA School of Advanced Leadership Fellowship and has also graduated from the AASA National Superintendent Certification Program. Mike was the 2017 Lake County, Illinois, Superintendent of the Year. He was the 2021 Loyola University Distinguished Alumni for the School of Education. He can be found on X at @mikelubelfeld. He and Nick Polyak authored the 2017 Rowman & Littlefield book *The Unlearning Leader: Leading for Tomorrow's Schools Today*. He, Nick, and P. J. Caposey authored the 2018 Rowman & Littlefield book *Student Voice: From Invisible to Invaluable*, the 2021 book *The Unfinished Leader: A School Leadership Framework for Growth & Development*, and the 2024 book *The Unfinished Teacher: Becoming the Next Version of Yourself*. Mike and his wife, Stephanie, have two children and live in suburban Chicago.

Nick Polyak, EdD, is the proud superintendent of the award-winning Leyden Community High School District 212. He is in his sixteenth year as a public school superintendent in Illinois. He earned his undergraduate degree from Augustana College in Rock Island, Illinois, his master's degree from Governors State University, and his EdD from Loyola University Chicago. Nick has been a classroom teacher and coach, a building- and district-level administrator, a school board member, and a superintendent for the past sixteen years in both central Illinois and suburban Chicago. Nick has earned an IASA School of Advanced Leadership Fellowship and also graduated from the AASA National Superintendent Certification Program. Nick runs international global service, culture, and leadership trips with superintendents and boards of education. He can be found on X at @npolyak. Nick is the 2023 Loyola University of Chicago Distinguished Alumni for the School of Education. He and Mike have co-authored four books, three with P. J. Caposey. Nick and his wife, Kate, live in suburban Chicago.